Ever Changing
Inside Outward

Rhonda K. Herring

Gazelle
PRESS

Mobile, AL

ISBN 978-1-58169-309-6
For Worldwide Distribution
Printed in the U.S.A.

Gazelle Press
P.O. Box 191540 • Mobile, AL 36619
800-367-8203

Dedication

I am no stranger to pain
I am no stranger to God

This book is dedicated to the pursuit of peace and joy
in a world filled with pain and sorrow.

To my mother...Because you are my mom and raised me well...
you are my hero...I love you.

To my brother Ray...from the sunlight, "I got my crown!"
I can see clearly now... See you in heaven.

To my sister...You are in a better place than I am...
I miss you.

To San...Your strength is impeccable.

To my husband...You stretched me, and I grew...
Thank you.

To *all* my children...I adore each of you...
Keep the faith.

Table of Contents

PREFACE

Life is ever changing. Thus, the name of my work: *Ever Changing*. Not exclusive to my life (my story), but in every life. If you are living and breathing, then expect the process of change to be evolving in your life— even when you are not aware and think everything is stagnant. As you change, my hope and prayer is that you will recognize this change and embrace it.

Change played a part in every iota of my life. It happened more so when I was unaware. The things I thought were a permanent part of being me were exposed as things I held on to selfishly. The things I thought defined me no longer defined me. Definition slipped away. I am today someone I never thought I would evolve into. Actually, I never thought of evolving into myself. How odd. But, it happened. I thought *I* knew me. But *God* knew me better. The process was not easy, and as you read through the pages of this book, you will see that I was a hard case. If it were not for my upbringing I would have probably strayed further off course. Thank you, Mother.

I had my genes, youth, upbringing, my teen years, and my young adulthood, and I thought I was in control and that was the very essence of who I was–good or bad. The bumps and bruises were just issues in life—move on. I was in control. Little did I know that it was not all about me, and every day I was getting closer to a life-changing experience. Every day, I was evolving into what God ultimately wanted me to become. The process was slow but sure; change always is. But it was definite enough to make me understand who I am and why I truly exist. My ideologies transcended into deeper purpose. I was ever-changing.

Lastly, I wrote this book at three separate intervals. The journey came first; I was compelled. Need I say more? This is a trilogy, as I like to call it. This is a group of three dramatic or literary works related in subject or theme: Ready or Not, Complicated Adjustments and Inside Outward. Three voices, one story, and one life changed. I hope you will find this a life-changing reading experience.

SECTION ONE

READY OR NOT

"Train up a child in the way he should go:
and when he is old, he will not depart from it" (Proverbs 22:6).

Introduction

In the beginning of my process of change, it came and did not care if I welcomed it or not. This section is the story of my upbringing and how important a role it played in my life. I would be remiss if I did not start from the beginning, although the memoirs came first. As I changed into adulthood, I thought I knew what I wanted. I thought I had what all young adults think they have—the right insight and perspective, and in the right order, mind you. This section demonstrates a youthful awareness of how life changes and how my life changed and how this affected everything. Change was happening, and I was simply reacting to the change, but with absolutely no direction. The purpose of the change was slowly being revealed, but my carnal eyes could not see.

CHAPTER 1

In the Beginning

You could say that I had a pretty good upbringing. Back then, I did not think about it at all. My world revolved around my mom, my sisters, my brothers, and our small suburban housing development. My mom told me what to be, and that is what I dreamed of becoming. She said things like, "There's not a person on this earth better than you, and you, young lady, are no better than anyone else"; "Work hard and do what is right"; "Do unto others as you would have them do unto you." She taught us to stand up for ourselves and what we believed in. She taught us not to be afraid of anything and the value of getting an education. For the most part, she showed us how not to give up, how to get back up again and again when you fall, and to keep going no matter what. She taught us that quitters never win, and winners never quit. She led by example. My mom never gave up, no matter how much she hurt, no matter how much she endured. She never gave up on us or on life. Of course, I did not realize this until I started going through my own life experiences. I just thought my mom was immovable, invincible, unstoppable, and tough as nails. Little did I know that even when you are all those things, life still hurts! I was and still am inspired today to have a mother like mine and so thankful for that upbringing.

My mother made me learn and recite the "Serenity Prayer" over and over again. This included before meals, at bedtime, and any other time it seemed appropriate. I recited it probably a million times in my young life. But back then, it just seemed like something that I knew and something that I said to get praise at dinner or to impress my mother's friends and to make her proud of me. Little did I know that it would play such an integral role in everything I did in my life. Little did I know that it would take me down and over the paths that were set before me. What is instilled in you as a child carries with you throughout your lifetime. It is what shapes our personalities, our drive, our character, and even our goals in life—everything.

My mother was a strong woman and did not tolerate much ignorance. She was a firm believer in discipline and appropriate behavior. I knew she loved us back then, and as I reflect back to those times, I know for a fact she did her very best to guide us in the right direction. Now, whether we always followed that direction or not is an entirely different story. My mother was very stern and authoritative (as am I), and when she spoke, we listened. She spent most of her time with us, working for us, feeding us, teaching us, talking to us, or playing games with us. I have fond memories of playing board games, jack rocks, baseball, kickball, volleyball, and watching television game shows with Mother. We loved *Ponderosa*, *Eight Is Enough*, *Good Times*, and, of course, our all-time favorites *Jeopardy* and *The Price Is Right*. These are just a few things we did together when Mom was not working.

Mom didn't date much, but a lot of times we ended up in the back seat at drive-in movies with her and her date. I remember once at the drive-in I won a huge jar of popcorn with candy hot balls (as we called them). The jar was about as big as I was. We were so happy. With five of us, it did not last very long, though. For a little girl, winning that was an awesome feat, and it is still one of my favorite memories. I cherish the fond memories, and still today we play Scrabble, Trouble, and watch *Jeopardy* together every chance we get.

Life as I knew it was good. Of course, we had our share of problems like most families, but we held it together and loved each other in spite of everything. We knew Mom would be there no matter what, and it felt wonderful growing up with such an awesome, supportive mother. There were times in my teenage years I certainly didn't appreciate her being there and setting curfews, but now that I look back, I am glad she did. I am glad she laid down the law and demanded that we follow it.

In the Beginning

I have been told and reminded many times of things that I do not remember or things that I choose not to remember, as someone put it. I guess these things are on the dark side of our upbringing. Maybe I have subconsciously blocked out the things I choose not to remember, but I am not sure. It seems so pointless in my life to ponder over things that I consider a normal part of one's upbringing, and even more pointless to ponder over things that supposedly happened that I absolutely cannot remember. Of course we were spanked, we got scolded, we had a lot of responsibility (cooking, cleaning, etc.), and no, my mother was not the sweet, permissive mother I would have liked to have had back then; but what matters most is that we were fed, clothed, and taken care of immaculately, and that is no lie. We were taught everything in this world on how to survive and make it. We had the best example, and that example still shines brightly in my mind today. This is what *I* know, and those are *my* thoughts and memories. I have pondered over my upbringing for years. Nothing bad happened, and my mother was the reason for that. She was on the case. That is why I think to this day I have been able to be the mother I have been to my children. Now, that is not to say that my mother has been perfect and certainly not to say that I have been perfect. I mean, I can remember sometimes when my mother yelled, fussed, and tore our behinds up. I can remember sometimes when I yelled too much, fussed entirely too much, and tore up some behinds myself. I guess back then it came with the territory. Although, I must admit I would certainly do things so much differently if I had to do it all over again, and I believe my mother would do it differently also. At this point, she probably would not admit that.

Discipline was not negotiable back then—not in my world, anyway—and bad behavior was definitely not tolerated. I did not appreciate it back then, and as I got older I really grew to resent it all. However, as an adult with children of my own, I know that discipline is very much lacking in this generation, and it is very obvious. I would say it contributes to over sixty-five percent of the issues we have with young people today. But some will say the way my mother and I disciplined was too harsh and that we stripped away so much from our young people. Now, for the most part, our children are saying, "I will never be such a harsh disciplinary as my parents." They are sparing the rod and definitely spoiling the child. Two generations, two extremes. Lord, have mercy.

I guess the only thing negative that I can say as far as my upbringing is concerned is that we grew up without a father. When I think about most of my friends and the other families in my world, the majority of us were fatherless. Therefore, I did not feel burdened down with thoughts of where the father figure was or where my own father was. He was a mystery man that came around occasionally and gave us a dollar or two and then disappeared until the next time we saw him. I do not remember calling anyone "Daddy," not even him. It is mind-boggling even now to think that as important as fathers are in children's lives, I had no thoughts of or longings for my father, or a father, or so I thought. Today, as a mature woman, I know that there had to be some kind of void there, but at the time it seemed so unimportant. Little did I know back then that just as things we are taught shape us, unfortunately the very things we have no control of also play an important role in shaping our very being. Imagine having genes and DNA from someone that you do not even know and possibly picking up traits and characteristics from this elusive "father." Imagine trying to understand who you are and why you exist and why you act and laugh and feel the way you do. Even though it didn't really seem to matter growing up, it did.

As I grew older, I knew there was something in me that motivated me—something that made me confront my issues and keep going. When I was a teenager, my mom always encouraged me and always told me how beautiful I was. I smile when I think about that, because I was horribly skinny and I also had a lazy eye. I had gone through two eye surgeries as a child, but neither completely corrected the problem. The funny thing is that it did not really bother me or stop me from enjoying my childhood, nor did it make me feel different from anyone else. I had my share of friends and grew up very outspoken. Sometimes I was too outspoken, and that brought my mother to school on several occasions to rescue me from myself. I really did not have too much of a complex about my eyes except when I was teased. That's when I would actually remember that my eyes were a little different from everyone else's. I cannot remember ever crying about my eyes, but I do remember getting my feelings hurt. But no matter what, my mother told me I was beautiful, and that is what I believed. The older I got, the less I cared about the name-calling, although it did catch me off guard most of the time when someone tried to insult me. But life went on. I had my share of puppy-love crushes and friends, and was always complimented and told I was pretty. When I looked in the mirror, I did not see what the others saw, I guess, and certainly did not see any type of handicap or anything that would keep me from being as confident and self-assured as anyone else.

As a junior in high school, I was nominated to be a debutante and attended some of the elite training classes that led up to the main event. But I dropped out because I thought all the other girls were snotty and all that etiquette training was for the birds. I think that was the first time I disappointed my mother. I loved tennis, volleyball, gymnastics, track, and basketball. I was an athlete and very competitive in sports. I still love sports after all these years. I was not thinking about the opportunities and exposure at that time.

I graduated from high school at age eighteen, and life went on. I really did not know what I was going to do with my life. I had a three-month-old that I adored. I brought a child into the world, only to realize afterward that the father and I were not going to stay together. The relationship with him seemed pointless to me, so I moved on. I got a job and started raising my daughter. Times were hard, but Mom was there all the time. She adored my daughter too. It was her second grandchild and first granddaughter. I really wanted to go to school and become a nurse, but that vision was slowly slipping away because I was a young mother working and taking care of an infant. The father was in college at the time and provided little financial support. He was my first actual boyfriend and my first sexual partner. I dated him for three years. When my daughter turned one year old, I officially broke up with him and started dating someone else. He was devastated, but I knew that as I had gotten older, he was not the one I really wanted to be with. Life as I knew it changed.

Things that didn't really seem to matter began to haunt me. For the first time in my life, I really began to worry about how I was going to raise my daughter. I worried that she would grow up fatherless like me and what that really meant. I began to wonder if not having a father myself had anything to do with me being so nonchalant about getting pregnant so young and about breaking up with my daughter's father. I also started to wonder about my father. I heard my mother talk about him and of course I saw him occasionally throughout my childhood, but I didn't *know* him or anything about him. My mother would often say that I looked and acted just like him. I did not know if that was good or bad or if it was okay or not. I actually did not know how to *be* most of the time, because I really felt uncomfortable when she said that. I did not know much about my mother and father, but I know that they were never married and he had other children. Sadly, I do not know my sisters or brothers on my father's side. My mother raised her children up as a tight–knit, close family, and we were all brothers and sisters, no questions asked. However, I knew that my father was also my youngest brother's father, and as for my other siblings, well, I really did not know who their fathers were.

Growing up, that never entered my mind, nor did I entertain any thoughts of that nature. But now, I began to question what I was doing and where I was going. It seemed I was going nowhere fast, and that I was going to end up with a dead-end job in a dead-end town. How could this happen? After all, I had so many hopes and dreams, but having so much responsibility at nineteen made my dreams seem unobtainable. All the changes in my life over the past year, graduating high school, having a child, and having to support and take care of a child made me afraid and anxious, and I began to worry. A lot.

CHAPTER 2

The First of Firsts

This became a very hard time in my life. It seemed my mother was disappointed in me, and I was disappointed in myself. I worked a job I did not like at night and took care of my daughter during the day. Times were hard. I was living with my mother at the time. I was dating someone new and had been for about a year. I was definitely looking for a way out. I had no clue as to what I was going to do.

However, the light in all of this was my brother. He was always there with encouraging words and would always tell me everything would work out. It was hard to believe, but I hung on to those words for dear life. They were all I had. He would always have a joke or some funny story to tell when I saw him, and I saw him often.

By that time, my older siblings had left home and moved from our hometown. It was my hope that I could leave as well. There were only my brother and my baby sister, who was in high school at that time, and me. I visited my brother at work and at his home and went to the movies with him and his family as much as I could. He was my hope, and he had such a positive, sunny outlook on everything. My brother was married and had two young children. He was a great husband and father, and I admired him so much for that. He was so young, but he seemed to know exactly what he wanted in life. He was so mature for his twenty-seven years. He was the light of my life and meant the world to me. I cherished the times we saw each other, and he helped me out on so many occasions—whether it was kind words or a few dollars here or there.

My boyfriend and I were serious by then, and although my mother told me he was very irresponsible, we were actually talking about getting married. We had decided that we would go into the military together so that we could at least get some good training and move out on our own and make a life for ourselves. We went through all the procedures and passed the tests with flying colors. I was going into the medical field, and he wanted to be an infantry soldier. The last step was getting a physical examination. We went through the examination, but I did not pass the physical because they found a spot on my lungs. The doctor called us into the room and said that the Army would not accept me because I had sacardosis, a lung disease.

My boyfriend left and went through basic training, and his first duty station was in Germany. I was hurt and did not really know what would happen between us, and at the same time I was afraid of what having sacardosis meant. The doctor told me I could have inherited the disease from one of my parents. I wondered about that as well and, of course, I thought of my father and how even though he played a very tiny role in my upbringing, his role as father in my biological makeup was important. Even though he was not physically present in my life as a child and a young adult, he actually *was* there and did play an integral role in what I was as a human being, in my genetic makeup and what I was developing into. He played a role in all my thought processes, in all the decisions I made, in my choices of men, in my personality, in how I looked, talked, walked, and what I aspired to become. He was not present, but he was "there." He had no part in raising me, caring for me, nurturing me, guiding me, financially taking care of me, disciplining me, or teaching me. But because he was my "father," he had a certain amount of control over my destiny, and that seemed so unfair. Some aspire to believe that the biological father is not important. I beg to differ.

After my boyfriend finished basic training, we got married and moved away to another state. I was so happy to get away and start some kind of future—anything other than the bleak future I was seeing for myself at that time. I was very sad to move away from my mother, but she was happy for me and had the same confidence in me that she always had and told me she knew I would do well.

By that time, I was getting to know my father, and we were spending a lot of time together. I cannot remember how it all came about, but one day he just showed up and showed an interest in getting to know me, and we went from there. I helped him out in his businesses at times, and we were getting comfortable around each other. I was really enjoying having a man that did not want anything from me. Although it did seem strange and I could not have possibly known what a real father was, I enjoyed the times we were together. He seemed more like a friend than anything else. He did not offer me any guidance, any words of wisdom, or even act like a father. We just basically did things together, or I would work in his club or at one of his car dealerships in our local community. He introduced me as his daughter, and that was it. I felt numb when he said that and would notice the awkwardness of his words and the questioning eyes.

I cannot ever remember feeling like I was his *real* daughter because to me, you just cannot pick up a relationship after twenty-one years and say, "This is my child," and have that child feel warm and fuzzy about it. I would just smile because that is what I do when I am in an awkward or uncomfortable position. That's what I do when I am at a loss for words. Some people giggle nervously and some people fidget, but I smile. As a matter of fact, it felt so awkward that I wanted him to stop introducing me in that manner because most people knew him in our community, and their eyes seemed to be asking, "Where did she come from?" Maybe I was just paranoid. He was a businessman, an entrepreneur, and I was proud of that for sure. You did not see that much in my small community.

Getting to know my father was like finding a new friend. As time goes on, you realize that you enjoy and value the friendship. I wanted to ask him where he was when I was growing up, what was he doing, what was he thinking, and why he did not come around more often. And most of all, why now? But I did not because I do not think I really wanted to hear his answers, and that maybe the truth would have been harder to swallow and the fantasy was easier to digest. Honestly, I really do not think he even knew. I never did ask or get the answers. All I did know was that he had something inside of him that wanted to get to know me then. I appreciated that.

I never did get to really know my father, but I was thankful to have had the time with him and to watch him, hear him, and see what kind of person he was. To me, my youngest brother definitely had his sense of humor and his openness, and what I got from my father must have been his looks because at that time I did not have much of a sense of humor, nor was I very open. I was complicated. My two sons definitely remind me of my father, and they have that wittiness to them as well. Genes—the gift that keeps on giving.

Shortly after my reuniting with my father, my spouse and I packed up all our belongings (which were not much) and moved to Arkansas. Life there was okay. For me, it mainly consisted of taking care of the children and getting used to the changes. I began to play the roles of wife, mother, and employee. This was the first time since I was grown that I felt security and a sense of some type of future and independence. Independence came with a price. We had children and a brand new life, and it was okay. However, mothers have such insight and wisdom, you know. My husband was very irresponsible, and that led to many issues in our marriage. He also was abusive at times, and he would drink alcohol more often than I care to even speak of. I had no education and two children at that time. I wanted and needed to work and found a job in a department store. There were ups and downs, but I was determined to make it and not go back home a failure.

One day shortly after our move, my mother called and told me that my youngest brother was missing. Missing? How could that be? My sister-in-law called the police immediately. My brother was everything to me. I enjoyed our relationship over the years, my other siblings and I were not really that close at that stage in our lives. We all lived in different states and did not keep in contact that often. My brother brought me much laughter and joy, and I marveled over seeing him every time I went home to visit. Now, what exactly did I hear my mother say—missing?

That night, I had a dream. It was the first dream I can remember that was related to a real live incident ongoing in my life. I dreamed that my brother came over to visit me and to do some work on my car. He was always working on my car, cleaning my car, or under the hood for some reason. He was all smiles, and in his own matter of fact way told me, "I know what is wrong with your car," and he lifted up the hood and stuck his hand down in what was an engine full of water and pulled out a part that had rusted and rotted from being in the water and said, "This is what is wrong with your car." I woke up suddenly and stared into the darkness. I was afraid, and I wept. I wept because I did not know what was happening. All I knew was that my sister-in-law said my brother did not come home last night, and to me something had to be terribly wrong. He was not that type of person. Where could he be, and why wouldn't he come home? He had never done anything like that before, and they had been married seven years. I wept because my imagination was going wild, and I was afraid. I was afraid because he had not come home and because of that dream. What did it mean? I was eight hours away from home.

I finally fell back to sleep and was awakened by the telephone ringing. My mother was on the other end. Day two, and he still had not come home. I told my mother I would come home that day. During the course of the day, the hometown news channel began to report that my brother's car had been found parked at a friend's house and that the owner of the house was missing and his car was missing also. Everything went blurry, and all I can remember is arriving at my mother's house and telling her about my dream and asking the family members of the other missing person if there was water in the area.

My brother was murdered, and his body was pulled from the river as my family sat in the living room watching the news. It was horrible. Words can never ever describe how unfair that was. My brother's body was identified by his childhood best friend, who had gone to the area where they had found blood on a bridge. Some young lady was arrested as a suspect that knew something and had taken the police to that bridge. My brother's best friend Myron identified my brother's body—not his mother, father, sister, or brother, but his childhood friend.

As we saw the police lift his body out of the river, the clothes could have been his: the shoes, the body, the height and the weight, the hair could have been him, but I was in disbelief. We had no warning, no call, nothing. We just watched. We all cried. I was in denial. I refused to believe that it was my brother. Even after the body was brought to the morgue, I refused to believe it. I had not seen the body, and I did not want to. I knew that it all *had* to be a lie. My brother could not have been murdered. Shot

13

twice? Why? Who? He was the kindest person I ever met. His heart was of gold, and he brought sunlight to everyone he knew. We all adored him. This was the first time I had ever lost anything or anyone I truly loved. This was the first time that I realized what real pain felt like. I did not like it. I felt so out of control. I had had my share of heartache and struggles along the years, growing up and in young adulthood, but this was a different pain and struggle.

We had to see the body. *I* had to see the body. I had to go with my mother and my other siblings. I did not want to. I had to go to provide moral support for my family and for his wife and my niece and nephew. But I just knew that it would not be him. I did go, but I said I would not look because it was absolutely without a doubt not him. My mother made me look. I walked up to the casket and looked, but I did not recognize him. I immediately turned away. My mother said, "Look again, closely." For a moment, I wanted to scream at my mother—something I had never done in my life. Just for a split second, I wanted to tell her to be quiet and to tell her she did not know what she was talking about, but as I turned to look at her, I saw the pain and sorrow in her face.

Being in the water for three days had distorted his skin coloration. His eyes were swollen from being shot in the head. I said, "Mom, it is not him. You are all mistaken. Let's just go home now." She said, "It *is* him. I wish it was not, but it *is* him." I did not respond. She put her hands over his swollen eyes, and I removed my hands from my eyes and looked, and it was him from the bridge of his nose to the bottom of his chin. He looked exactly like our father. I looked at the hair, and it was his hair. It *was* him, except for the eyes that always had that mischievous boyish I've-got-a-secret quality. They were swollen and closed, never to open again. I wept. They arranged the funeral because it was surreal to me. I was no help. I walked around in a daze. After the funeral, I stayed at my mom's house for several more days, and every morning I was awakened by her cry. I had never ever seen or heard my mother cry. Each morning, it started out as a low whimpering and ended up as a loud cry like some kind of wounded animal. We were all wounded. We were torn apart. I did not know how or what to do. I wanted to give up—I honestly did. It was not fair. Who would do such a thing? It seemed that my emotions shut down, and I withdrew deep within like a butterfly in its cocoon. I think I subconsciously vowed to never love that way again to protect myself from ever feeling that kind of hurt and pain again. This was something new, something unfamiliar to me—like a foreign object entered my being. I felt devastation. I felt helplessness. I felt out of control. I did not understand; I was in denial. I could not believe that another human being could do this to another human being. I had heard of incidents where similar things like this occurred, and I saw things on the news and on TV, but never for one moment did I think it could happen to *my* family. I was not raised to expect this type of thing, this type of occurrence, or this type of tragedy.

As the days passed, they arrested the young lady who led them to the bridge where she said the bodies were. Her mother convinced her to turn herself in when she found traces of blood on her daughter's clothing. She had participated in helping her boyfriend get rid of the bodies. She helped him tie cement blocks to both my brother's legs; they then drove to the bridge and threw his body in the river. Apparently, she did not participate in the murders, but she did help him get rid of the bodies and also helped destroy the evidence. That is what they charged her with. She got ten years in prison with the possibility of parole in five years. She was very young. I still wonder what kind of woman would do such a thing. I am not sure if I agree with her sentence, but we did not appeal. At that time, our focus was more on the person who did this crime and finding him.

The man was found approximately seven days later, hiding in his mother's apartment in another state with the stolen Cadillac. They found him four days after they arrested the woman. They found blood in the car—my brother's blood and his friend's blood. The seatbelts were cut out; I guess he had to cut the seatbelts out to get the bodies out of the car.

As the news was reported to us, we were even more devastated to know the details of what had transpired. A random act? No. The man worked for my brother's friend and had plotted to rob him and steal his car (the Cadillac) that night. My brother showed up to visit his friend that he had known for only four months. The man who killed my brother testified and wrote in a statement that he "did not know the 'other guy'." My brother was the "other guy." The culprit just wanted the Cadillac so that he could drive back to his hometown about six hours away. I guess he wanted to drive back in style. My brother was just the "other guy" who got in the way of his plan. Cathy's husband and Laura's and Little Jack's father was the "other guy." *At least call him by his name*, I thought, *not just the other guy!*

He took his life, and still today I know that he cannot remotely comprehend what he did to us—to my brother's wife, to my brother's two children, to my mother, to me, and to my other siblings. My brother died without knowing our father. His children would grow up not knowing their father. No matter the reason, two more children would grow up not knowing their father, and their father never knew his father. Ironically, the murderer had a son, and he would grow up without his father who would be in jail for a long time. The reasons totally differ, but the result was the same. No matter the reason, the need was still there. Life can be so harsh.

There was a trial, and I came back to put an end to the tragedy because somehow, no matter what happens, there has to be some type of closure. If there is no finality to a circumstance, the circumstance and the dynamics of it can overcome normalcy. It was horrible, and the person that killed my brother was horrible and showed no remorse. He had no father present, only his mother. She admitted to riding in the car. "Didn't you see the blood and bloody newspaper, ma'am?" the district attorney asked. She insisted she did not see anything and rolled her eyes. Her demeanor was not pleasant; I was not surprised. I will never ever understand his mother, yet my heart goes out to her. But I thank God for the other mother, for if she had not convinced her daughter to turn herself in, the murder might have never been solved. It would have probably been investigated locally and closed.

He was convicted with no opportunity for parole at age twenty-four. My brother was only twenty-seven. During his testimony, he still insisted on referring to my brother as the "other guy," even though he had to know his name by now but did not care to use it. Maybe it was because he did not know him or because he obviously did not place any value on his life. That made me so angry.

We cried throughout the trial. We saw all the pictures. We saw his family and his small son. We even ended up in the bathroom with some of the woman's family. It was very awful. We heard all the gory details. We held on to each other because it was the first time we had experienced such pain. I went back home after the trial, broken and not even knowing how to go on. I'd shed a lot of tears in my life, but this was the first of firsts for me. As a result, my family became closer. I spoke to my other siblings often, and we realized then the importance of family and keeping in touch and just calling to say, "I love you."

Almost twenty years later, my daughter found information on that person and sent me a link to the website. I got on the site and saw the picture of the killer. I know it was him, but he was twenty years older than when I sat across from him in that courtroom. He was so very young when he committed double murder. I did not realize that he was the same age as I was. That shocked me, and I wondered why I did not realize that then. He had aged a lot, and it looked like he had had a rough time. There were dark circles under his eyes, and I stared directly into his eyes for the first time. During the trial, we looked at him, but the pain did not let us see a human being. The only thing I saw then was an animal—an animal that would do it all over again for personal gain if he had to or if he had the opportunity. We looked at him but did not see anything but blankness in his eyes. Each time we looked at him, he would move his mouth as if to say, "Yeah, I did it. So what." It got to the point that we eventually stopped even looking at him. We had never ever met anyone like that. We were all in shock. He never showed any type of remorse during the trial. It was exactly as it was, and he just did not seem to care. I guess that is why he got double life and fourteen counts of armed robbery with no opportunity ever for parole.

Twenty years later, I looked just to see if I could see some sign of remorse or some sorrow or sadness. Aside from the flaring nostrils and a stare into the camera, I saw no indication of either—just the same blank stare I saw when he was twenty-four. I wondered what was behind the eyes. He is forty-four now. I felt nothing. I read that he had nine infractions while in prison and that at this time, he was in some special confinement away from all the other inmates. I wondered what happened and why he was even now in consolidated confinement. I did not feel any compassion for him or any sympathy that he had spent twenty years behind bars. I was surprised because normally I have compassion for everyone. But for him, I felt nothing.

I remembered he had a son when I saw that he was a "Sr." I thought

17

about his son and how my nephew grew up without a father, and so did his son. I wondered where his son was and if he knows what his father did. Did he visit him? Those answers I will probably never know, but I still wonder. As I stared at him, I noticed that he looked mean or was trying to look tough. I guess he is tough because of the awful and cruel thing he did to two human beings. I wondered what kind of childhood he had. That is when my compassion came into play. I know that one day he was a baby and he had to grow up. I wonder what he saw or went through that would make him capable of one day committing such a horrendous crime, murdering two people, tying cement blocks to their bodies, and dumping them into the river. I wonder if he thinks about what he did. Does he have any regrets? Would he change things? Has he been tortured by the memories of murdering two innocent men? I thought of what my brother went through, of what he probably was thinking when he realized that he was in danger. Did he beg for his life? Did he cry? Scream? Did he think of his family? I am sure he did. But we know for certain that he did fight back. That was obvious with all his wounds, but he died from a gunshot to his head. He wanted to live. Lord, have mercy!

As always, we somehow got past the hurt and pain and, as they say, time has a way of healing. I will never forget. I will never, ever understand, but I thank God for the precious memories of my brother. I can smile because all I know of him is goodness. But as I smile, I think of my oldest and only brother left. I think of him and the irony of the vicious cycle that I see. He did not know his father either. Why are these fathers absent, and why in the world are the children suffering because of their absence? I ask God what is going on. How do we break this cycle? Then I realize that the devil is busy and comes to kill, steal, and destroy in every form, shape, and fashion. Whatever it takes, and if it means the absence of the fathers, then so be it. It makes the devil's job so much easier, and we allow it. We, as women, in our choices of mates who we allow to father our children and men who do not take their responsibility seriously and put their selfish needs before the children. We somehow are failing. Most of the time, the fathers that are doing this grew up fatherless themselves. Even with the fathers that are in the homes, it is not enough to be there in the home and feel self-righteous because you are there, with no relationship with the children—no care, no guidance. It is the same as not being there.

We have such responsibilities to our children, and we cannot take parenting lightly. Fathers, stand up and take control of your minds, your thoughts, and your actions! Everything you do will affect your children. Can't you see? Love, care, and guide them in the way that they should go so that they my not stray away; or if they do, they will eventually come back. They need you and your love and your correction. Correct them now with parental love, and then others who do not know them or care for their worth will not have to. To the many fathers that are there and participating whole-heartedly in the upbringing of their children, we recognize you and thank you. You can confidently say that you are a "real man." My God bless you.

I never had a relationship with my oldest brother. My oldest brother is about six years older than I am and left home when I was about twelve years old. I have some fond memories of him. He was so smart and is probably a genius. He never carried books to school but always made straight A's every year. I remember asking him how he did that, and he said emphatically, "I read the books the first couple of weeks of school." I was amazed at what he said, and it must have been true because he never carried books after the first two weeks of school. But as I said, he always made the A honor roll every year, every reporting period. He was an honor student.

I also remember him doing the local daily newspaper crossword puzzle, and he did not miss many words. We all played along with *Jeopardy* each night, and I cannot ever remember him missing too many questions. He could have been whatever he wanted to be because he had the intellect. After graduating from high school with honors, he immediately left to serve time in the Air Force and stayed away for about seven years. When he came back, something was different about him. I was nineteen then with a daughter. He did not stay in close contact with us while he was in the military. He just left and then reappeared seven years later. Even today, I do not know what happened. I know I love him, and one day I hope to have a relationship with him. He is my brother. I wish I could fix all the years that have passed, but I cannot. I can only hope that his future will be brighter. For some reason, I know he has suffered tremendous pain somewhere down the line. I wish I could fix that also. As I sit here, my heart breaks for him because he is brilliant, and somehow something or someone broke his spirit.

He will not talk about it, but I remember his smile, his brilliance, and I know that life can be cruel and that we must keep everything in perspective—the good, the bad, and the ugly. If we do not, then one day we will just lose hope. My hope is that one day God brings my brother back to our family. At this time, my brother and I do not see each other, and he is almost completely isolated from our family except for an occasional phone call to my mother. No one knows why or understands, but that is something we all deal with every day. What could cause so much pain that an individual would just give up? Maybe someday, he will talk about it and let it go. I pray he does. As for Jack, he has his crown. May God bless my oldest brother and all the other men out there who are struggling.

CHAPTER 3

Affairs of the Heart

A year later, we got orders to go to Japan for two years. I was relieved and welcomed the change. I was moving on with my life at this point but still licking my wounds from the year before. I never felt much support in the loss of my brother from my spouse, so I really did turn inward and never discussed my brother much or even talked about him with anyone. Even today I do not, and even now as I write, I weep.

I felt really alone and did not like going back home to visit. The pain of my brother not being there was almost unbearable. I would always feel so sad and think of him and how things would never be the same. I relived the loss every time I packed the kids and myself up to visit. It was hard enough as it was. Some days were harder than others, but even more so when planning a visit. I told no one—I just suffered silently. I had mixed emotions; I wanted to see my mother and my sisters and the rest of the family, but there was a deep sadness just knowing that he would not be there. For some reason, I just did not think even my family understood. We did not talk about him much, and when we did, I brought him up and then everyone told their own stories of their remembrances of him. I just listened as if I had none of my own. They were private to me. I guess I was selfish and thought he was *my* brother and nobody cared about him like I did. I know now that was not true, but that is how I felt. That was my own limited thinking. I was so young, and everything was all about me.

I can remember having a conversation with my oldest nephew years later, and we were discussing the family. We were talking about Jack, and my nephew said that he thought his mother and Jack had the same father. I was shocked that after all these years, he did not know that Jack and I were the only two siblings that shared the same father. So, I gently told him "No, it was Jack and I." As I looked at it, we had the exact same genetic makeup, and I had lost the only sibling I had that was just like me. It was a huge loss because then I began to realize how important those things are and how much they play an active role in who you really are as a human being. Growing up, that never really made a difference to me, but at that time, it did. In that instance, it really made a difference because that made me feel like there was no one else in the world left with the exact chemical makeup and genes as me.

Loneliness set in all over again. But of course that was my own limited thinking, and it made me feel like the world owed me something. I loved my other siblings, and we became close and are close today, but like I said that was my excuse to say, "Woe is me" at the time. That was also before I met my brothers and sisters in Christ.

After my brother's passing, I did not see his wife or my niece and nephew that much because during the trial and the testimonies, division came between my sister-in-law and us. At the time, we did not agree with a lot of what she said and how she handled my brother's funeral. She did not want the casket open during the funeral and would not allow their children to come to their father's funeral, and we all thought that it was wrong of her. They were so young then but still... As I reflect back, I lost so much, and in the midst, I also lost a niece and nephew and a sister-in-law.

We really did not see them or play an active part in their upbringing. I was young and blamed my sister-in-law for a lot of things, although now it seems ridiculous. It is funny how you rationalize things when you do not deal with your own pain. You start blaming others, and I blamed her and did not care to see past my own hurt to even begin to understand her loss. I do today. Back then, though, I only thought of myself and how deeply hurt I was.

We did see my sister-in-law and the kids from time to time, but it was never the same. I know I blamed her for us not seeing my brother's children and also for what happened. They never moved away from the area, but I still did not see them even when I went home to visit. My family had moved to Japan by then and stayed for five years. I saw them on rare occasions after we moved back to the U.S. My mother did not see them or my sister, although they were just miles apart. I never understood that, but I was so busy trying to get my life together that I never even proposed the question. I think it had to do with my sister-in-law being very religious and not celebrating birthdays or any holidays. I would ask my mother from time to time, and she would say that they came by on Thanksgiving, and that would be the end of the conversation.

They grew up without our family being a part of their life and without their father. I used to say that it was all her fault because of her strict religion, but today I know we all share our fault in that. I lost my brother, my niece and nephew, and my sister-in-law that fateful day. They lost their father and a grandmother, aunts, an uncle, and cousins that fateful day. My sister-in-law lost her husband and his entire family. Lord, have mercy!

The children are all grown now, but the division is still there. My nephew is really trying to get to know us, and we are reaching out to him desperately to make up for the times when they were there but we were not, or we were there and they were not. I used to say it was because I lived so far away, but I know that is an excuse. I allowed that division to get between my brother's family and me. I am so sorry I did and missed my niece and nephew's childhood and teenage years. Even now, I do not know them, and I feel the void tremendously. This happened because I was selfish, bound up, and I did not understand what love and caring was all about.

As I said, we relocated to Japan shortly afterward and extended our tour of duty for three additional years. I had my third and last child overseas. My marriage was okay. I was so busy trying to raise the children and trying to get adjusted to having a new baby and living in a foreign country that I did not have time to really think about much else. My spouse was still drinking heavily and being his old irresponsible self. I was tired, trying to raise three children and work a full-time job. The only thing good in our marriage was that we shared the responsibilities of the children, took them everywhere we went, and shared the household duties. That helped a lot, and I never really felt overwhelmed with children and housework.

I started to work when the baby was about ten months old, although I wanted to wait until he was two years old. But I did not have much of a choice because as the result of drinking, my spouse had gotten into a bad accident and almost killed himself. The night he got into the accident, we had some friends over and had prepared dinner. We had a good time. We were young, and I always liked to have friends over and to play the "happy hostess." We laughed and talked and ate. It was nice. By then, we could afford to entertain a little and do more things, so we enjoyed ourselves, and our friends would always bring food and, of course, alcoholic beverages. I would like to have had the get-together without the alcohol, but to him it was a necessity. A party without alcohol? Go figure. The kids were always so well-behaved that we would get so many compliments on their behavior. They would do their little socializing, and most of our friends had kids their age, so they would eventually go to their rooms and play Nintendo and/or watch a movie or something.

We did not socialize into the wee hours of the morning because our friends worked just like we did. Most of the time, we would start around seven and by ten everyone would have left. It was the time after the guests left and he was drunk that I dreaded. Sometimes, he would be all right and just be a little intoxicated, and we would clean up and get the kids off to bed and have a nice night. But on the nights he was drinking heavily, it was almost always an argument about something that was said or something I did or did not do. On the night of the accident, he was determined to go out and get a beer because all the beer was gone. He had already been drinking, and I knew he would be driving under the influence. That is another thing I could never understand. Why he would drink and then drive? Did he not care about his life or the lives of others? I would ask him that, and he would say that nothing was going to happen and that he was not drunk. But I know that sometimes he was so drunk that I would be amazed he even made it back home. Not only that, he was a soldier, and if he got caught driving under the influence, they would take his license and reduce his rank. We definitely did *not* need for any of the above to happen. He had made rank so easily and was doing very well in his career. But there was something inside of him that made him reckless, out of control, and willing to risk his career, his family, his life, and the lives of others just to have a drink. It was the disease.

He would want me and the kids to ride with him sometimes after he had been drinking. But I would not ride with him or allow the kids to ride with him, and that would start an argument. I was in a no-win situation. But I could not take that risk; it was not in me. I did not want anything to happen to him, the kids, or anyone else. That was a battle that I would not let him win, and on those occasions I would fight back until he stormed out of the house or gave up and went to sleep. I knew about consequences, yet he threw caution to the wind more times than I care to remember. I know it was the disease that overtook him. After all, I knew we were very important to him, and he showed all of us that—when he was not drinking.

Getting back to the night in question, he was so determined to go to the store and buy some more beer. I did not want him to go. I just had an uneasy feeling about it. Although he was not sloppy drunk, he had had a long night before, working twenty-four hour guard duty, and had not slept but a couple of hours that morning. It was the wee hours of the next morning, meaning he had only slept about two hours in a forty-eight hour period. We had gone to the zoo earlier that day with friends, and he had not slept. But he would not listen to me when I told him that I did not want him to go. I literally begged him to get some rest and told him that he could go tomorrow, but he insisted. He left. He didn't come home that Saturday night, and I did not hear anything from him all day Sunday. I told the kids their father had duty; they went on being the happy-go-lucky kids they always were.

I was suffering and knew something bad had happened. I was too scared to call anyone or contact his unit. No one contacted me. After the kids went to school on Monday, I packed our ten-month-old baby and went on-post. As I entered the gate, I saw one of our friends who was in the same unit he was in. He grabbed me by the arm and asked where I was going. I told him I was going to get groceries at the Commissary. He said, "Don't you know what happened Saturday night?" I said, "No," and demanded he tell me what happened. He said, "Your husband got into a car accident and almost killed himself." I stopped and stared at him at least a good solid minute. He did not say anything else for a moment, and then he finally said, "I am on my way to the hospital. He has been asking for you." I cried. I thought he was dying.

As I went to sit down, another friend saw me and told me that my husband was in serious condition and that he had some serious injuries to his head and hip. He said that he had already had one operation and maybe he would have to have another. I was in shock. I began to talk and tell our friend that he didn't come home Saturday and that I was too afraid to call the company. I rambled on and on. And that is why I came on–post—to see if he was there. I did not know what was going on. We called his wife (who was my friend as well) so that she could pick up the baby and get the older kids after school. Our oldest kids were nine and seven at the time. She got the baby and said for me not to worry about the other kids. She hugged me and whispered, "I thought you knew."

We got to the hospital in about an hour and a half. There he was, lying there all bruised up but alive, and I wept again. I could not believe this had happened, although I knew in my gut that something like this was going to happen if he did not take control of his drinking. I had begged him to stay; he would not listen. I even opened the window as he walked to the car and said, "Please do not go tonight." He answered, "I'll be right back." I stared out of the window for about ten minutes after he drove off and then slowly closed the window.

Now this. I was glad he was not dead and his injuries were not as serious as what I had been told. He hurt his hip and was on crutches and had glass in his head that they had to remove, but he did not damage any major organs. He would be fine. He was happy to see me and held on to me so tightly. He apologized and vowed to never drink again. I believed him. It was a single car accident; he fell asleep at the wheel from lack of sleep and being intoxicated. The car was totaled, and when I saw the car, I wept because I could not understand how he was able to walk away from the accident alive. I was glad he had, and so was he.

He was released from the hospital a few days later and returned home. Then the ramifications of driving under the influence set in, and again it affected the entire family. He was reduced in rank and had to pay lots of fines, and his salary was reduced by two grades. It was devastating to our finances, and we had to move on-post. Although he was reduced in grade, they allowed us to move on-post anyway. Not only that, but we also lost the one and only car we had. So, when the baby was ten months old, I set out to work because we had to pay the bills and feed the children. It was a hard time, and aside from one very special friend, I was basically lonely and hurt and in a bad situation.

My spouse stopped drinking for a while after the accident (for about six months), but after that he started to drink heavily again. This time, I was finished with the situation. I just could not love him the same again. It took a lot out of me, and it showed me that even though he cared about me and the children, his problem was deeper than us. After he started drinking again, he was nastier than before, and it was awful on the nights he got drunk. He did not start out drinking every weekend, but he would get drunk at least once a month. I wanted him to stop and to get help, but he refused to acknowledge that he had a problem and did not realize that he was destroying our marriage. After about twelve months, he was drunk almost every weekend, and most times I had to walk on eggshells around him. I was sinking. I was sad, and I did not know how to get out of the situation I was in. I felt trapped in the marriage, trapped in a foreign country, and trapped in a job I absolutely hated. I was angry. I was angry inside. How could this happen to me? Why were we suffering because of his habit? This is not what I expected my life to be. I wanted better. I wanted out.

I finally decided that I would look for a better job—a clerical job. I had taken a typing course while I was pregnant and could type exceptionally well. So, I decided to start applying for secretary positions rather than working in the mess hall. At that time, KPs (Kitchen Police) that worked in the mess halls overseas were civil servants. So I continued to go to the personnel office and look for jobs in the clerical field. Finally, after about two months, I landed a secretary position and changed jobs immediately. I was promoted twice in two years, and really enjoyed the job and being a civil servant. I knew that I would retain my status when I returned to the United States because of the new Executive Order signed by the President that gave military dependents job preference at their spouses' next permanent change of duty station. I was very excited about that and about working for the Federal Government. At that time, I had obtained a General Schedule Five pay grade and was going to get promoted to General Schedule Seven the following year.

Unfortunately, things were not going well at home. My spouse was still drinking heavily. I was unhappy with my home life and my marriage. The children were getting older and getting involved in our arguments, and the arguments were getting more and more intense. I was trying to be a good mother to them, but I was very sad inside. I tried to hide it. This is a part of me that I have always had to deal with—being honest with myself—and sometimes even today I have to really do some soul searching to accept the realities of my life. I went on from day to day pretending that nothing was wrong. I guess I was hopeful that the marriage would survive and that we would live "happily ever after." After all, I did not want to get a divorce. Divorce was something I had never considered.

I cannot say that the entire marriage was a waste. We had the kids. That was a blessing, and I know I loved them and enjoyed having them. They are what kept me going. When my spouse was not drinking, our relationship was bearable. He was kind and gentle for the most part, and we had a good relationship together and with the kids as long as he did not drink. He also had a problem with blowing money and buying expensive things. It was money we did not have to spend. So we were always struggling financially, although I did work and we both had decent salaries. I wanted nice things, too, and we had nice things, but sometimes we would get ourselves in heavy debt to have those things.

We went through totaling a vehicle and not having a vehicle for about six months. I had to take the train to work every day. Believe it or not, some days I cannot remember how I got back and forth. I worked about thirty minutes from where we lived. If it were not for the train and friends (angels), I would not have made it.

During that time, I met a guy that I almost had an affair with. He was younger than I. We never slept together. I said *almost* had an affair, but we had the biggest emotional affair that any two people could ever have. We just did not have a sexual relationship, although we came close on several occasions. We cared for each other. I guess he was far away from home and lonely, and so was I. It was not something sleazy; it was something that brought us through a difficult period. He was young and lonely in a foreign country, and I was young with too much responsibility and no outlet. It was not something to fulfill a sexual need or something for excitement. It was something deeper than that. It was something I have honestly never felt before, nor do I ever expect to feel again. It was a case of someone put into your life for a reason, and it is okay because they are there for you to see you through a difficult season.

He was different in so many ways. He cared. He listened, and I know he shared my pain. He wanted to protect me, but he could not, and sometimes he would just hold me so close to him like a real father would do his little girl to protect her from her fears. He never asked for anything. I am sure if he has children that he is an excellent father today. He would listen to me so intently. He knew me down to my very core; he knew me better than I knew myself. He encouraged me to go on, and he honestly gave me hope. He listened to me about my children; I shared with him the highlights, I shared with him about my family, and I shared with him about my husband and our rocky marriage. He listened to me and helped me make the decision to have my tubes tied. It was him who I consulted, and he eased my fears. I knew at that time I did not want more children, and my spouse did not want any more children either. I came home after the procedure, and it was this friend who saw me through it. My spouse did not talk about it, nor did he understand the depth and meaning of what I went through as a woman making the decision to have her tubes tied.

My friend accepted that my tubes were tied and that I could not have any more children. He said it did not matter to him at all. He just wanted what was best for me. He wanted me to be happy and wanted to be the one to make me happy. Even after he knew I could not get pregnant, we still did not sleep together, although we could have without any fear. We did not, and he told me that he would never ever ask me to do something like that while I was going through so much with my spouse. He said he did not want to complicate my life and that he just wanted to be there for me. He would say, "We will have all the time in the world for that when the timing is right." I could not see how the time would ever be right, but we were definitely emotionally involved. He was there for me at some crucial times in my life. I often did not go straight home after work so that we could spend some time together, especially after a horrible weekend of arguing and fighting. The funny thing is that my spouse never asked me where I was or never complained. He always was sober and with the kids when I got back home.

Although we chose not to sleep together, it was very hard not to. He was very kind, considerate, and loving. I knew he cared, and I cared for him. We would go out to eat, to the movies, sometimes just sit in his friend's car and talk, dream, and hold each other. We always worked something out, and we continued to see each other for about a year. I talked to him on the phone as much as I could. We talked for hours and hours at a time while my spouse was hanging out. I saw him as much as I could. He was there for me more than my spouse even wanted to be. He was always available and waiting for my call. He was always running to my rescue when I was hurt. He wanted me to leave and go back to the States. I would not. I did not want to leave him, but I did not want to keep going through the drama in my marriage.

My father passed away while I was overseas, and my spouse honestly did not seem to care at all. He was not close to his father, and he knew that I grew up without my father. However, he did support me wanting to attend his funeral, so he escorted me back to the States. I appreciated that. He would tell me how he could not remember his father ever playing with him, throwing a football with him, or even buying him anything (shoes, clothes, toys). That seemed so sad to me, and I thought how sad that must have been to have a father at home that was just "there." It somehow seemed even sadder than not having a father around at all. I knew why my spouse drank so heavily; that was his only remembrance of his father. His father was an alcoholic. My heart went out to that little boy who watched his father drink when he needed him to father him, to show him love, and to spend time with him. Sometimes I would weep for him because I knew that he must have had some serious issues with that. So, he drank just like he saw his father do in order to forget, I guess.

I was very sad that my father had passed away before I could return to the States and spend more time with him. He looked so young, and I just stared at him lying in his coffin throughout the service. I was sad because I did not know him better, that the children did not know him at all, and that life was such that I was born and raised without him. I did not quite understand, and I was old. At that time, I decided that I would do everything in my power to keep my marriage together and allow my husband another chance so that we could raise our children together.

At the funeral, I saw a lot of people who I thought resembled him and me. I looked around, and it was amazing to me. No one introduced me to these people at the funeral, but I faintly remembered meeting some of them when my father introduced me to them prior to me moving away. I said goodbye to my father, to someone I really did not know. But, he was my father.

I decided also that seeing my friend back in Japan was not something I would continue to do. I needed to concentrate on my marriage and helping my spouse through whatever it was he was going through. I decided that I had to convince him to get help and that we would seek some type of counseling together. When I returned, I told my friend that I would not be able to see him again and that I had made a decision to work out the issues in my marriage. He was devastated, and so was I. We hugged and said goodbye. We held on to each other and looked at each other a long time before we left each other. I had made up my mind, and I knew it was only right because we were getting extremely close, and it was getting in between my relationship with my spouse. I began to not care where my spouse was or what he was doing. I only wanted to talk to my friend on the phone or to go visit him when I could. I was preoccupied with that most of the time. We finally said goodbye, and we both agreed that it was for the best. He said he understood and only wanted what I wanted.

CHAPTER 4

Saying Goodbye

I did not see my friend anymore for about five months. But one day, he came into the office were I worked. He did not talk to me. He asked another lady in our office something and turned and walked out. He did not look my way, but I knew why he came in. He just wanted to see if I was still there. I watched his every move. He was so graceful in his movement and so suave in his mannerism. That is what I liked about him: he had such a gentleness about him. He was smooth, he was honest, and he was what I really wanted, but he was not my spouse, and I was married. He had no children. He was about five years younger than I was. He had his entire life ahead of him. He was an officer and a gentleman. He would make someone a great husband, and he would be a great father someday. I wanted to run behind him and tell him how much I missed him, but I just sat there and watched him go. The ladies in the office said how good-looking he was, and I smiled inside and said to myself, "You do not even know the measure of that man." For about two or three weeks, I expected him to come back or be standing outside waiting for me.

Life went on, but I thought of him often. I missed talking with him and being with him. But I went on to concentrate on my spouse, who did everything in his power to resist any of my help. No matter what I offered, he resisted. He did not want my help. I tried everything. I tried talking to him about our relationship and our issues. He saw no issues. He would always say that he would stop drinking and that we would be okay—that he could stop drinking anytime he wanted to. He just did not see anything wrong with drinking and that he could control how much he would drink. He would say that he was sorry for the arguments and what he was taking me through, and that it would not happen again. Eventually, the fighting stopped for the most part because he would just get drunk or high and fall asleep.

It was a lonely period. For a while, it was okay; I just welcomed the peace. But then he began to hang out, and I did not know where he was. I was concerned about where he was most weekends, and some weekends he would not come home at all, or he would come home drunk and would sometimes start an argument. So, I never knew. He'd gotten his license back and believe it or not, he began to drive drunk again. That began the serious demise of our marriage. We had about eighteen months left of our five-year tour overseas. We had agreed to extend our tour of duty to five years so that we could get back on our feet. I was ready to go back to the States. I was tired of living overseas and not seeing my family on a regular basis. We both were homesick and decided to go on vacation and return to the States to visit our families. During this period of planning, it was a happy time because we both looked forward to visiting. We did much better in those two months prior to going on vacation, and I thought maybe we would be okay and that the vacation would help.

The time came when we would leave, and we were all excited. When we got to the airport, I could not believe who I saw—my friend. It had been a year since we had decided not to see each other and six months since he had come into my office. We looked at each other—no. We stared at each other. Every opportunity we had, we were looking at each other. I was wondering if he was returning to the States permanently, and he was wondering the same thing. I tried to be calm. I tried not to look, but I could not help it. My spouse was there, and so were the children. He smiled at me every time our eyes met. He watched me and my children and my spouse. He smiled at my youngest son and talked to him when he tried to stray away. My son was three years old then. He had never seen them before, but his eyes said he knew my children; I had shared everything about them with him. His eyes said he approved. He saw my spouse too for the first time as well. I saw him look at him and then look away. I guess it was hard because he knew so much about him, and it wasn't good. I was ashamed of that. He stayed in that same spot where we could see each other. I felt uncomfortable, but I wanted to see him. I watched him interact with his friend, whom I also knew. I wondered what he was saying to him. His friend glanced over at me. I did not move either. I wanted to know if he was leaving for good and if so, where he was going.

Finally, I took my oldest son into the arcade, and he came into the arcade where we were. The first thing he said was, "I miss you so much." I looked over at my son; he was engrossed in the game about three feet away. I looked out to see where my spouse was. He was still at his seat with the other two children. Their backs where turned away from the arcade. I instantly said, "I miss you too." He said, "Are you leaving?" I said, "No, just going on vacation." I found out he was just waiting with his friend to pick someone up at the airport. He was not leaving either. He said, "Call me when you come back." I said, "Okay." He gave me his number and walked out. He was there when we boarded the plane, and I turned and looked. I could not resist. He smiled. I turned away and got on the plane.

We stayed in the States for two weeks. I enjoyed myself and my family. I enjoyed my spouse, and he was kind and we did a lot of things together and spent a lot of needed alone time while the children enjoyed their grandparents and cousins. Time went by so fast, and before we knew it, we were preparing to go back. I do not know if my spouse was afraid I would not come back and that was why he was so attentive to me those fourteen days. I was hoping that this would go on and the drinking would stop. We got on our flight and returned back to Japan.

We were back in Japan for about a month when my spouse started back drinking and hanging out. I knew it was just a matter of time before I would call my friend anyway. I guess I used my spouse's drinking as an excuse. I called my friend, and we talked for about three hours in the wee hours of the night. He said that when he saw me at the airport, he was so afraid that we were returning to the States permanently and that he would never see me again. I told him I felt the same. He told me flat-out that he loved me and that he wanted to be with me forever. After all I had gone through, I knew that I loved him too. But I knew that it was so unfair to him that I had lived so much of my life and he had not. He had never been married, nor did he have any children. He said again, "Your children are my children. They are beautiful." I laughed because my daughter was about twelve, and he was about twenty-five. We talked about how much we missed each other. We talked about what we went through. He confided that he would come to my job and just wait for me to go to lunch or leave work to go home. I said, "You should have said something." I told him I looked for him everywhere I went on the installation. We talked and spent as much time as possible together after that.

Six months later, his tour of duty was over, and he returned to the States permanently. Of all the things for him to return to—family, friends, and even a possible girlfriend—he still wanted to stay in contact with me. He wanted me to leave as well. He was concerned about the children and me. He said he would write to me every day until I returned to the States. One week after he got back to his hometown for vacation, he wrote me a long letter. I guess the last time I saw him I was so upset I mixed our home APO address up with my work address, so the letter came to my spouse at *his* unit instead of to me at my office. How ironic.

The day my spouse got the letter, he called me at work and told me I needed to come home right away. I had no idea what was going on. I found out when I got there. I read the letter. I could not deny what had happened; it was an emotional affair. The letter was beautiful and confessed his undying love for me and how he missed me and he hoped one day we could be together. He talked about how he wanted to do so many things and how he regretted us not sleeping together, but he knew that one day we would be together when the time was right. He also wanted to stay in contact with me and said he would write to me every day until I actually left my spouse. He did not want me to do it for him, but for my children and myself. He often told me that it was not healthy for the kids or me.

I knew all of this, but I still stayed because I did not know how to get out of it. I did not want to fail. I was a winner, not a loser. Isn't that what Mom told me? It was the competitor in me. It's always been there, even as a child. I wanted to win. The tennis match, the basketball game, or the board game—I tried hard at everything I competed in. I definitely was an athlete and could have done well in a number of sports. But the main reason was I did not want to go back home with three children and no job. I felt there was nothing there for me and that I had a better chance of making it by just staying where I was. I knew that the decisions I made to have children and get married early (or was it carelessness?), were the result of my own choices, and they were my own responsibility. I was brought up to be responsible for my own choices. I was taught that the choices that I made were mine, and I had to live with them and take responsibility for them. It is called *ownership*. I did not have the luxury of going back home to Mom with my tail between my legs. That is probably what a lot of people thought would happen, but I knew that I would not do that. It was not an option. After all, where would I work?

I was already a civil servant, working for the Department of Defense, and that was the bright light in my life. I was learning a lot of good, solid computer skills, clerical skills, and interpersonal and office management skills. Although I did not know it at the time, it was the means wherein I could take care of my children and myself. My friend always told me that he would take care of me and the children and that I always had a place to go, but that was not possible. That is what his letter said. He said after returning home and getting settled, he found he could not get me off his mind. He said that of all the things for him to do, he found himself doing nothing and decided to write to me two days after returning back to the US. He was sincere—the most sincere person I had ever met in my life. When I decided to get my tubes tied, he was right there telling me that it was the right thing to do, but he was sad because he knew that if we ever got together, we could never have children together. He was hurt, and I knew he was; it was not a game to get what he wanted. He was too well put together to pretend. He wanted what was best for me. I survived that part of my life. He cared so much more than my spouse did. We discussed everything so much more than my spouse and I did. It was not my spouse who helped me make decisions I had to make. It was my friend.

We walked together and rode the train together and held hands everywhere we went. He was so handsome and so mature, even moreso than myself with three kids. But it was time to let go, and that was the end. I never looked back. Even today, the memories make me sad, but I have to smile. I have no regrets; he was my guardian angel, and if it was not for my guardian angel I cannot imagine how I would have made it through that period of my life. God was there, and I was unaware. My spouse licked his wounds and threatened me for about six months. I vowed to never contact my friend again. I wondered for years what he thought about me never writing him back, and I know that it hurt him deeply. I wished I could have at least let him know that my spouse ripped the letter up and I did not have his return address. I was hurt, but I kept going on. I worked and took care of children and the house, and tried to make the marriage work. So did my spouse for a while, but then he went back to his favorite pastimes—drinking and drugging and blaming me for everything.

I was thirty years old, and the kids were growing up so fast. My daughter was twelve years old, and my oldest son was ten. I remember thinking to myself that I would not let my children go through what he went through because it could have the same effect on them. I knew that his abuse of alcohol and drugs would be the reason that one day lead to the demise of my marriage.

CHAPTER 5

On My Own

We stayed in Japan for a little over a year. We enjoyed the tour, and I really liked my job and being able to buy some nice things and to help take care of the children. We had fun sometimes. The marriage was not a complete waste, and my attention was actually where it was supposed to be again. It had been an emotional year, and it was nice to not have to keep that kind of a secret. Although my friend would always come to my mind from time to time, and I would feel the loss, I knew that it was something that could not happen because I was married with kids, and he was young with no ties. He needed someone like himself. Deep down, I knew that would not have been fair to him.

When we got orders to go back to the States, we were assigned to Fort Huachuca, Arizona. I had spouse preference, so I retained my civil servant position and my pay but lost a couple of grades. I started working two weeks after I arrived and actually had to take my son (who was four at the time) with me on the interview. He was so well-behaved that my soon-to-be-boss said that he knew I would be able to handle the architects and engineers with a well-behaved little toddler like my son. He said, "I know that you will be able to handle those engineers and architects with ease." At that time, I was interviewing for a secretary position for the Director of Public Works, editing specifications for eighteen engineers and two architects. I was very happy to be a secretary for those important people and worked there three years before getting a promotion.

After returning to the States, I wondered why I was in such a hurry to come back. I missed my family, but we did not see each other that much unless I went back home. Our marital problems carried over to the States. No one knew what I was going through, and I never told any of my friends. I had quite a circle of friends by then, but I was almost always the listener and kept my woes to myself. I have always thought that my issues were really not that important since I grew up as the "knee baby," as my mother called it, this meaning the middle child. To me, that meant, "Okay, you are not the baby, and you are not the oldest, so get in where you fit in." It was always about either my baby sister or about my oldest sister and seldom about me. But I was a fighter and fought for my attention. I probably acted up the most just to get some kind of attention. I wonder if it is like that for all middle children. We become the mediators or the go-between or the peacemakers, never really understanding where we actually fit in, but just making our way as best we can. Even today I am a listener, and for the most part, am uncomfortable when people make a big deal over me. I also do not like attention that much and would rather just fade in with the crowd most of the time. Not that I do not value myself or have low self-esteem, I just believe that everything is in the Masters' plan.

Through a lot of self-reflection and all that listening over my life, I learned to love myself and appreciate the gifts and talents God gave me with dealing with people. I really did not get to understand them for a long time. But it is an absolute gift to put others before yourself. It is a gift, but a painful gift to bear. Only someone who is called to do this can survive it. Sometimes, you want to say, "Hey! What about me?" but you are genuinely more concerned about the other person. But at the same time, it is a gift that is so rewarding. I can truly say that I am not selfish, snotty, arrogant, egotistical, self-centered, or stingy, and am always happy for others and try so hard to love everyone and treat them with respect. Funny, though, most people do not know this about me until they really get to know me. I am very reserved; only in my later years have I really come to speak out. The one thing that I now strive so hard to do is let what comes out of my mouth be acceptable in God's sight, although sometimes I fail miserably.

Of all the good things that I tried to be, I think that my spouse used those things to his advantage. He knew I wanted the marriage to work because I am a very devoted person. For many years, I tried to make the best of an almost unbearable situation. My spouse was not that bad when he was sober. As a matter of fact, then things were really nice. I really liked him as a person. He was always playing with the kids and cooking and cleaning, the same as I was. We spent lots of time together, had a very active social life, and took the kids on picnics and to the zoo. Basically everywhere we went, we had our kids. We had some good friends, and we socialized quite a bit. The socializing was always nice as long as my husband was not drinking. I dreaded the times he was drinking, and for the most part even though he said he would not drink, he always ended up drinking, ultimately getting drunk. That's when the problems began. It was as though he turned into a totally different person. He became harsh and critical and would sometimes embarrass me so much. When we were at home, he would sometimes turn violent in a moment's time. I often had to leave the house until he fell asleep or call the Military Police. That was so embarrassing, but no matter what, he still continued to drink. The Military Police would take him to the barracks and release him the next day. The next day, he would be sorry, and I would be angry, and our ritual would begin again. He would promise to stop drinking or at least stop drinking so much, but within the next month or so he would be at it again. I would do everything I could to make us a normal family, and no matter what I did it only lasted but for a time.

I often thought of his father and mother. I was afraid that I would turn into his mother. She was afraid of her husband, and he would try to beat her and curse her out when he was drunk. He didn't care where he was—in public, in front of us; it just did not matter. I felt so sorry for her. He pulled guns out on her at times. I remember my spouse trying to take a gun away from his father so his father wouldn't point it at his mother or quite possibly even shoot her. I was afraid I would turn into her. It was like a disease with him, and as hard as he tried, he could not beat it. It would always win. Now I understand it was a disease, but back then I was young, and there was not so much openness about alcoholism and drugs as is the case today. He was just like his father, whom I had watched destroy himself, and my mother-in-law and my spouse and his siblings did nothing. It was taboo to talk about. They never tried to get any help for him. They just ignored the problem. As much as my mother-in-law suffered with his disease, she never talked about it either. But she always looked so tired. I told my husband that they should try to get him some help, but they never did.

Today he is in a nursing home and is very ill. Alcohol has destroyed his body and left him a very sick man. My mother-in-law eventually moved out of their house about five years ago, and she now lives in an apartment in my hometown. No one lives in that house now, and when I go to my mother's house, I always look at their house. My ex-father-in-law lives in a rest home because he is too sick to live alone. He will not allow her to take care of him, and I guess he will probably live there for the remainder of his life. (This is after forty years of marriage.) I always feel so sad about that because after all she went through with him (and, boy, did she suffer a lot). Their marriage ended up like that. We must pray for marriages, old and new.

I was afraid I would end up like her. But something deep inside me would not allow me to accept that kind of abuse. I valued myself a little more than that. In the end, I would often fight back when my spouse pushed me too far. I was tired of it all. His mother would cry and run and scream and hide. I did not. I would fight back, though now I know it was wrong, and the kids would cry and probably think, "Oh my God, they are going to kill each other." The thing is, he never gave me a black eye or any physical bruises. But he would from time to time have visible scratches.

I would always remember him telling me that he could not remember one thing he and his father ever did together. My heart went out to him, and I would always forgive him and try to show him love and take care of him. But he was self-destructing right before my eyes. Unlike his family, I talked to him and pleaded with him to get help. I brought home pamphlets, etc. But nothing seemed to work. Even today, I know that what I did was right when I asked him to leave so the children and I could go on with our lives. I filed for a legal separation in October and my spouse left the military and left me and the kids at Fort Huachuca. I mean, he literally walked out. He left me about $2,500 in the bank and a check for about $3,800 and that was it—it was over. I was on my own. I went to stay with a friend, and that was disastrous. A week later, I moved into my own apartment for the first time in my life. I was completely on my own. I was afraid and excited at the same time.

The one thing I did know was that I was not going to take him back and that I was not going back home to my mother. I had a good job with great benefits that I needed since I would lose all my military benefits. I moved into a nice, safe neighborhood, and life went on. The kids were getting older then; my youngest son was eight, the oldest son was fourteen, and my daughter was seventeen. I had gone through too much over the years, and I knew that I could not take any more disappointment. I just wanted to go on with my life, and I did.

I had just gotten a promotion and retained the grade position that I lost when I had returned from Japan. The pay was okay for that time, but my bills were overwhelming. I was out there in the world alone and did not really know what to do. I had been so wrapped up in the military lifestyle that it seemed like I was in a foreign country again. I had lived on-post all my adult life, shopped at the commissary and the Post Exchange, and worked on-post. That was the bulk of my adult life. I rarely went off-post for anything except to go to the local mall. I knew where the mall was, and that was it. I slowly began to learn the area and get acclimated. My kids were still going to school on-post, and I had to get them registered within the local school system—decisions, decisions, decisions.

It was very uncomfortable being single again. I had never been single in my adult life, and it didn't set well with me. I enjoyed the companionship of a spouse. I enjoyed the joint ventures and the joint responsibilities of taking care of a family. But now it was all on me. I resented that most. I continued to work and took care of the kids every day. They were not real young, and besides, I had a seventeen-year-old daughter who could help. But, oh my God, she was no help at all. She was bossy and irritable and probably thought that I was the dumbest woman on the planet. We had our times. Again from my upbringing, there were certain boundaries you just didn't cross. Talking back was one of them. She often crossed that boundary, and we would go at it. I refused to let her run the household, and she refused to allow me to have one moment's rest when she could not have her way. At the time, I didn't look at things as I do now. I did not look at it as a time in her life when she was growing, maturing, and actually changing. I looked at it as sheer rebellion, and I wasn't going to allow her to bring turmoil into the household. I wanted some peace.

On My Own

I was tired, disappointed, and up to my neck in paying bills. I needed a change and a promotion to meet my obligations. I considered finding a job outside of the Army. Every time I looked outside the Defense Department for a position, the pay was less than what I was making, even with my best administrative skills. Having no other recourse, I decided to go back to school and finish my education. I enrolled and started back to school, embarking on something that I never dreamed would be so demanding. I continued working, taking care of my family, and pursuing an undergraduate degree.

Some days were easier than others, but deep down in my heart I knew that education was something that I needed. I'd known that for years but somehow always got distracted with either a pregnancy or some other need or diversion. Out of desperation, I took on three courses most of the time, and it was not easy. Finding time to study was hard. I lacked the discipline, and most of the time I was just too tired after working eight hours and sitting in a classroom trying to pay attention for four hours two or three nights a week. I struggled trying to handle all the responsibilities and then educate myself. I had some resentment with my ex at that time because he was nowhere to be found. He offered no support financially, nor did he even visit the children for long intervals of time. I kept on going, though, somewhat unaware that I was being carried instead of making my own footprints in the sand. Still, though, I reached the point where I simply had to let something go, and I did—my children. I actually spent more time away from my children than I should have. I was so busy trying to take care of them financially that for the most part, I believe I did not provide the emotional support they really needed at the time. After all, they were going through changes too. They were children of divorce. My concern was mainly for my youngest son who was then only eight or nine. But I was wrong in this also. The older children were fifteen and seventeen and really needed me more than my youngest son did then. I was unaware and thought I was doing what was necessary. It might have been okay if I had had support from their father and if he would have continued to play an active role in their life. Only he chose not to.

My grades were really good, and I maintained a high GPA, but it cost me. I was tired and grumpy most of the time and, of course, lonely. As the days went on, I became very lonely and wanted to find a friend. I did have close male friends, but no one that I desired to have an intimate relationship with. I went out on a few dates, but it was nothing serious—a couple of flings here and there, but nothing to actually write home about. I was reluctant to get seriously involved with anyone because I just didn't have the time, and I was afraid that it would interfere with all my responsibilities.

I had gotten saved back in 1992 and was trying to reconcile what exactly that meant. I was dealing with that issue as well. I had gone through a divorce and was struggling financially and emotionally after giving my life to Christ, and I wasn't feeling warm and fuzzy about that. I thought getting saved meant that everything would work out. However, I continued to go to church faithfully and to listen to tapes and songs. As I listened more and more, I really began to gradually pull myself away from a lot of the pain and sorrow, and I began to realize that getting saved was definitely one of the highlights in my life. Now there was something that sustained me—the Lord. Even in my darkest hour, I still felt a ray of hope. I still had that determination to go on. I never faltered in going to church or reading my Bible when I could. I began to get strong in the things of God. I was not living right now, but there was a stronghold over me to learn and hear about the things of God. I had my favorite radio ministers, and I remember listening intently while driving to and from work, and to and from school. I remember sitting in my car late at night after class, feeling too tired to walk up the stairs, and listening to the Word as it was being preached. It motivated me, and I was seriously seeing a change in myself—a change that I know was not of my own doing or a change that I consciously made. I was the same person and doing basically the same things, but the inside of me began to change.

One way I began to change was that I began to embrace the things I dreaded. I began to see a light at the end of the tunnel. I began to be joyful, and there was that inner peace that I could not even understand myself, let alone try to explain to anyone. When everything seemed so wrong, the inside of me could not identify with it. I could not understand. When everything seemed so bleak, I still had peace. Then came the conviction. When I acted any other way than acceptable in the sight of God, the conviction came. I could not identify it as conviction in the beginning. I called it failure—failing God and myself. Sometimes, it was so intense that I felt condemned and thought surely I could not still be saved and a child of God and do or say some of the things I did. I did not feel worthy.

As time passed and I began to grow in the knowledge and wisdom of God, I realized that there is no condemnation in God. I became familiar with and accepting of conviction or with God's way of dealing with his children. God does not condemn us. Why? Because of His Son Jesus Christ and what He did for all of us on Calvary.

CHAPTER 6

Struggles

As time passed (approximately three years), I was still working for the Department of Defense, Army, and had been introduced to a nice young man. I dated him for about one year before we got married. He did not have any children and said that it certainly did not bother him that I did, and life was good. I knew it would be okay because I really loved him and I really thought he loved me. He gave his life to Christ one day during a church service, and I was in heaven. It all seemed so wonderful. Or so I thought.

Finally, I had a mate—a saved man who did not drink or do drugs and who attended church on a regular basis. He was handsome too. What more could I want? When we got married and started our life together, I had so many high hopes. I was saved and he was saved, and God would work it out, no holds barred. We started off fine the first couple of months, and then there was a U-turn in the middle of the street. I began to see the real Jonathan stand up. All the loving and kind ways were zapped away. All the holding hands and attending church together were suddenly gone.

My children went ballistic also. They changed on me. They began to be conniving, unloving, rude, and determined that this man was *not* going to come into their home and take over their territory, meaning me or the house. What they did not realize is that they owned neither. At the same time, Joe (as everyone called him) was determined that they were not going to make his life hell, so they went at it. My daughter was the ringleader of her two younger brothers. Joe would enter the room; a hardy laugh would ring out as he left the room. They would not do what he asked them to do and often said, "You are not my father." What they did not realize was that for the most part, they did not have a father any longer. I just did not realize the void it had left in them. But they certainly did not want it to be Joe. I loved Joe, and my kids made me so angry most of the time because of the way they acted towards him.

After a while, Joe began to take it out on me—not speaking to me because of something they did, etc. It was crazy. I was about to pull my hair out. Time was passing, and my daughter eventually graduated and left home to go to college. She and her stepfather never reconciled their differences. So, I struggled trying to help her with her tuition and keep her in school; Joe refused to help. By then, we had moved and bought a house, and our finances were tight. I began to get child support eventually, and that helped out a lot. My oldest son eventually left home and joined the Marines, but not without some priceless memories. I loved my kids regardless, but I was glad when they could venture out on their own.

Well, being the man that Joe was, he never forgave the kids, and the marriage continued on its rocky course—up and down worse than any roller coaster. My youngest child was six years younger than my oldest son, so he was just really getting to middle school when his brother left home. He was twelve years old.

God blessed us in so many ways, but we just could not get the children issues together. We both made pretty good money and had a beautiful home in one of the most sought-after neighborhoods. But our house was not a home. All three of us were miserable. The sad thing about it was I was happy before we were married, and so were the kids. A lot of years passed, and nothing really changed. Finally I knew that I had to leave and let go. This time *I* left. This time, it was me who walked out and took my child and moved on. The divorce came a couple years later. I never looked back. Two marriages, two divorces, I was not proud.

CONCLUSION

As the months and years went by, my life began to drastically take a new direction, and a deeper sense of awareness evolved. I had a vision and a compelling desire to start a journal of memoirs, but no revelation or known purpose—just to keep writing. It felt better; it kept me focused. I had no one to talk to, so I started talking to God. I turned to my heavenly Father, and the most important relationship that anyone could ever have began. Finding that relationship helped me reconcile my relationship (or lack thereof) with my own father. I began to heal in that area and to realize that a lot of my choices and decisions stemmed from the pain of not having a father and the denial of my need. I began to experience what it was like to have a father through my relationship with my heavenly Father. I opened myself up and accepted His healing. I needed to be healed in other areas as well, so I allowed God to heal me one issue at a time, one step at a time, and the journey toward wholeness began. I learned to trust in Him and to rely on Him for wisdom and guidance. Therefore, I began to grow and mature in the things of God.

SECTION TWO

COMPLICATED ADJUSTMENTS

"Ain't no rock going to cry out in my place!"

Introduction

Section two of this book is my memoirs—unaware, but faithfully writing and capturing the journey toward maturity and ultimately absolute change. Absolute? Yes, but don't be misguided—not perfect. We sometimes are unaware of what direction we are going and resist changes. Through this journey of change, a bold account (a testimonial) was being revealed. I was unaware, but God was in control and directing every step. The journey brought about my significant change. Resistance came sometimes, and so did disbelief (which God helped). It was an emotional roller coaster. However, it led to much-needed change (as you will see) in thought, character, perception, insight, understanding, and wisdom. I would like to call it "following the call on one's life." This is the journey of one life that changed toward betterment, toward the good that preserved a life and the good of the almighty sole purpose of the almighty God.

I began, "to read this is to understand the true meaning of life, love and the pursuit of happiness..."

February 13, 1992

To God be the glory, Christ saved me from myself. He washed away my sins. I am heaven-bound! Liberty: The condition of being free from restriction or control.

October 28, 1998

Holy Spirit, guide me!

Putting my thoughts down in a private journal has come and gone over the last few years. I feel this is something God wants me to do. I am overwhelmed this moment that I purchased two journals for that reason. God is good! I love the Lord! He is worthy. I have no plans on what to write at this time, but with God's help and the Holy Spirit's, I will be guided. All I know is that Jesus came into my life, and I have not been the same. I'll start the next time telling about me—how God has changed and is still changing me. Until next time...Rkh

November 2, 1998

I heard a wonderful message yesterday from Y Franklin (if I'm not mistaken), on November 1, 1998. It was awesome. It is amazing how people led by the Holy Spirit can make and interpret the passages so articulately. I just sat there, like always, in awe of God's ability to speak to His people through others. I don't know. I can't describe how I feel when I realize his awesomeness. It's like I am not even inside myself; it is like all feeling, thought, knowledge of me is gone. I feel so light, so at peace.

Paul and Silas in jail—singing and praising (when two or more get together, God's Word says He will be in the midst). The prisoners listening to them singing and praising God were set free, and their chains were loosened. Now when I first heard that, I thought that they were physically set free from their chains. However, when you really think about the text, it could mean that they were set free physically or spiritually or both.

He also talked about the spirit of the python who wants to squeeze the breath out of churches in these last days, where God's people will be bound and not praise and worship to their full ability. In relation to Paul and Silas, even though they were in jail and their circumstances appeared bleak, they still chose to praise and worship God. In the midst, they were set free physically and spiritually, and so were all the other prisoners and the guards. It was God's awesome power.

Sometimes I wish I could live in a church with the Holy Spirit right in the midst because outside the walls and outside of praise and God's anointing, there is reality. "How far is heaven?" sang the Hall Sisters. I long to be there to be in Jesus' presence forever, but for now there is reality until Jesus comes back for His people. His people...so many say they are His people, but then where does all the neglect, selfishness, anger, jealousy, envy, and strife come from? God is not the author of confusion. It is so hard sometimes. I know that I have my own faults. I am not perfect. I just ask God to renew in me a clean heart and a right spirit. My desire is to worship God in spirit and in truth. I know the unsaved need the same chance I got before I knew God. Sometimes I want to scream, "Don't you know that if you allow God to change your life, if you used to lie, cheat, steal, commit adultery, be envious, or fornicate, God can change your life so that you will not desire to do those things again?" God, don't they know that every person can change and be a new creation? It does not come easy. God knows I have a long way to go. Just having the desire to do right and trusting in God is the beginning. I always ask God to help me be a light and to help me make a difference in someone's life so that they can make that change. However, the decision is ultimately up to the individual...Rkh

November 4, 1988

Hi. Well, things are okay. Work went okay today. I was not pressed that much. That's always nice. God is forever working things out. The way I feel does not matter anymore; He always put me back on the right path. He always brought me back to the right frame of mind. God is awesome. Just think how we feel with the little responsibility we have. Think about God's responsibility keeping so many fragile minds together. As long as I keep my mind on Him, I know everything will be all right. This morning, my husband (I have not mentioned him yet. Well, introducing the leading man,

Joe (which is short for Jonathan). I have been upset with him for a while now. Not really upset, but I am disgusted with him. It seems we are just settling down. The fire we used to have is just an occasional flicker. But I've learned about feelings. What are they? Who goes by those these days? Tomorrow is another day. God is the only stability in my life. My other relationships flourish and die, flourish and die. That is why I keep my hand in God's unchanging hands. As far as my husband, I am totally committed to that man, and on top of that I am in love with him. When I prayed about him before I met him, God must have said, "Okay, you prayed for this. This is what you want. You asked for it; you got it." If the feeling is mutual, I cannot say. But, as I always tell him, we have committed now so just pretend. I do. The joke is really on me because I do not have to pretend—it was truly love at first sight.

God taught me how to love unconditionally—agape love. Okay, God. Why did you teach me that and then give me a mate that really has no concept of what unconditional love is? I guess it goes back to the "You asked for it; you got it." Be careful what you pray and ask God for. I just sit and wait for God to make that kind of love mutual between us.

Oh, I got a part-time job, thank God. I need it. I am excited. It is at the mall at the Information Center, and the pay is $6 an hour. I love working and assisting other people and just talking to different people. I am sure I will enjoy this. In my permanent job, I really do not get to do much customer service. It is just that the pay is not good at all. But it will help pay the bills and help me get my daughter through college. Love, Rkh

November 5, 1998

I just prayed to my God. I have been in His awesome presence. I can tell Him so many things. I know He already knows. This afternoon is not a good one, but just as Paul, I am at a place where I have learned to be content in every situation. I pray that I can be like Paul, though. Paul suffered so much. The things I suffer do not compare to what Paul suffered. I suffer in my marriage. I have been for a long time, God knows. But maybe everyone suffers. Marriage is not easy. I think my sufferings are at my husband's hands. I know he is suffering, and I don't know why, but I do know that anyone who can inflict so much pain on someone has to be in lots of

52

pain themselves. He goes to church each Sunday and has a Christian radio program on the local radio station. As long as I have known him, he has gone to church, but yet the pain and suffering is still there. He has not been set free—not filled with the Holy Ghost. I am not even sure he wants to be. He cares nothing about anything I care about. I wonder why he married me. I am sure he does too. I am no prize, and I have plenty of faults. I am definitely my mother's child, but I do know how to love. God taught me how to love. Just knowing how much God loves His children and what He sacrificed teaches me about true love. I thank God for that. I never want to be the person I used to be. I have been there and done that in my first marriage. I pray to God that I will experience that love from another human being (particularly my husband) one day. That has to be a beautiful relationship. I thought I had that, but being stupid, blind, and ignoring God's words and the most important relational scripture in the Bible ("equally yoked"), I married because of my own selfishness. I prayed and prayed, but I heard and saw what I wanted to see. I knew His Word, but I married someone who does not have a personal relationship or love for Jesus Christ. We are unequally yoked. I pray that one day, he will find his way and truly accept God in his heart. I only tried to do what was right.

I never want to see things as they truly are. I have struggled with this all my life. But when I think about it now, how can a person who will not accept God, who will not acknowledge what Jesus did for us, understand or believe the things of God? Therefore, how can they truly love themselves or anyone else? They must be born again, changed, and matured in God. There is my answer.

That is why he can treat me any way and not even consider how I feel. That is why he can pretend to feel good about himself or even think he feels good about the things he does. He allows the devil to use him. How can two Christians have no love, peace, and harmony in their relationship and in their home? Or, how can one Christian love another Christian who does not know how to love and does not desire to even try? I pray that God will help me to see things as they truly are and give me wisdom. If I can hear from you, God, I'll know what to do. Speak to my heart, Lord. Help me just rejoice in the expectation of your arrival. Rkh .

November 9, 1998

Hi. I had a long talk with Jesus and told Him all about my troubles. He said He is a way-maker. I believe Him. I felt sad when I woke up this morning. I did not feel like talking, so I did not. I did not call my husband all day, nor did he call me. I do not want to talk tonight either. I keep thinking how important decisions are and how we must keep God in the forefront of all our decisions. We must consult with Him in everything, and we must listen for His answers. Often, we consult with God, but all too often, we do not listen to Him. I keep wondering how I can get through to my children at ages twenty-two, nineteen, and thirteen when I, at age forty, made this decision. Live and learn and live with. It's a hard pill to swallow, but it's the hard truth.

It would be pointless to go into how selfish, unconcerned, uncompassionate, rude, mean, and cruel my husband is at times, for I know that I, too, can be that way at times. The difference is, for the most part, I am not. I love Jesus too much to feel that for more than ten minutes to an hour. God will keep you. I know He has been keeping me through this mess. Sometime I resent the whole marriage. I feel like walking out. If I do, it will be as if I am not trusting God with my life. God, I am praying that my husband and I will be equally yoked soon. I knew better, but I did it, so until God fixes it, I must learn to be content in every situation like Paul. Thank you, God, for your arms of comfort, your feeling of love, your peace, and your hope; if it wasn't for that, who knows where I would be—maybe Divorce Court again. Rkh.

November 17, 1998

God! I read or heard something awesome the other day. Speaking of love—a person who does not know the things of God cannot possibly give a God kind of love. What a revelation. I heard it before. I've said it before, but all this time I am seeking a God kind of love and will not get it until others know and love God for themselves. What have I been thinking? That applies to every person on earth. We look so hard for love and acceptance when only God and the people of God can unconditionally give a God kind of love. That is why the Bible says that we should not be unequally yoked. If we go against God's Word, then we will suffer unneces-

---

sarily. Powerful! I truly was blessed by the above. Well, anyway things are okay in spite of it all, and maturity in God is no joke. No matter what I go through, I would not trade God for all the silver and gold in the world. My relationship with Him is more important that anything in this world. I believe that because this is between you and me, and these are my deepest thoughts. God I love that. I thank You, God, for always being with me. Holy Spirit, thank You. Jesus, thank You for making all this possible.

My husband is going through hard times at work. I know that there is a reason for it, and I know that only good will come out of it. There are lessons to be learned, growing up to be done, and a maturing we all have to go through when we have a relationship with our Father. Trials and tribulations come to make us stronger. I hope this will make him stronger and more aware of himself and his actions. Please, God, help both of us grow closer to you each day. Bless my husband, whom I love with the God kind of love. Bless the children. Help me be what I should be to all of them. I plead the blood of Jesus over all of them and ask that Your angels be encamped around them wherever they go. Also, little D.J. Goodnight, Rkh .

November 21, 1998

When we walk through darkness, God's principles have not changed. God operates on the same principles. Remember: God is with us (Genesis 39:2-4 and 21-23; Psalms 23; Psalms 193).

God always has a purpose for the darkness we go through. God will reveal His purpose. God doesn't allow things to happen to us unless it has a purpose in our life. (Genesis 45: 4-8). God thinks from back then to here and on. God has a purpose for everyone's life. Don't focus on the darkness—focus on God. "Why the darkness?" we will ask. He will not answer when we ask; it will be when and in His timing. God speaks to us when we are listening. Listen carefully. It is worth listening, even if it takes a thousand nights. God will show us what we need to know to encourage us. He is working out details in our lives. God will not tell us when; God knows better. God has never failed to keep His word.

He will only keep us in darkness until He fulfills his purpose in our life. Get under God's will and purpose. God is with us throughout our lives, from the beginning to the end. We learn more in the darkness than we do in light.

Always walk toward the dawn of a new day, in total glory of God after we come out of the darkness. Live one day at a time. In dark times, we are always headed toward a dawn of a new day. Learn to listen to God. There is always a new light.

Those things we learn in the darkness, we must share in the light. What He speaks in the darkness, we will speak in the daylight. Share what you have learned in the darkness. Tell someone.

You must be a Christian. If you are not, then you are walking in darkness. God's children walk through darkness, and God walks with them or carries them through to lead them to their purpose in life. Hallelujah! Rkh.

December 3, 1998

God is watching your character. Can God trust me? Spend time working on yourself. Give up who you are now to become someone better. Someone's opinion of you does not have to be your reality. Can God trust me with favor? Oh, have I mentioned my husband's coping mechanism? Well, it is moving out of our bedroom into the spare bedroom every time he cannot have control of everything and everybody. He has moved out of the room again. I care, but I don't know what to do. It seems every time things seem to be getting better (well, to be honest maybe I only *wish* they were getting better), something happens. He said I wasn't doing my share, that it isn't half and half. But I thought I was doing more than enough or all I could. It seems *he* isn't doing *his* share. I pay half of the house note. I think that is more than enough. I buy all the food, pay the medical, and contribute what I can. He doesn't understand. He wants to have full control and be the man, yet he expects me to take care of it all. He has a whole room and bathroom that he keeps under lock and key. This is supposed to be *our* house now, and he expects me to give him exactly half of the house note. He wants to put his foot down. This is mine, mine, mine, and what's yours is mine, mine, mine. He has a spiritual problem; selfishness, self-absorbency, and greed overcome him, and he shows it often. I almost lost it when he acted so foolishly about the little cake he bought at Kmart. He had this "My cake, my cake... I bought me, me, me a cake" attitude. When he saw that my son had cut a piece of his cake and did not eat it, he wanted me to make my son eat it. But my son did not like the cake—what part of that does he not understand? That was the beginning of this argument. I wasn't going to make him eat it point blank. I watched him devour and hover over turkey salad—turkey I bought. I bought all the food for Thanksgiving and watched him eat it up for fear that someone else would get some. He ate Thanksgiving like he contributes. What happened to his half philosophy?

Trouble comes for our education. I must be an educated fool then. When I came home from work today, he had taken the big TV and moved all his clothes into his private suite in our house where I pay half the house note. This house has never felt like home. He managed to spoil that by locking up a room (the biggest bedroom in the house other than the master bedroom) that one of the other kids could sleep in and a bathroom. My sons are sharing a bedroom, which is the smallest bedroom in the house. It shows how much he cares about my children, like they really care anyway. They see him as I do—sad. They don't understand him and have never been through anything like this before. They probably wish he would just disappear or go crawl back under the rock he crawled out from under. I am angry and being ugly. He thinks he is hurting them, and honestly he probably is in some ways; because they thought he cared and cared about me, and they welcomed the marriage in the beginning.

My kids are no angels, but they are peace-loving kids and do not disrespect him unless they think I am being mistreated. Even then, they are only acting out of fear for me. They do not intervene unless he is actually trying to physically hurt me. He has done that before, and the kids had to intervene. I am so sorry I brought them into such a mess. The sad thing about it is I don't know how I got into the mess in the first place. Be honest—it was lust! If it was not for God in my life, I know that I could not go through this. I am really considering leaving. This is a house, but it is definitely not a home. We are just occupants paying rent so it can appear that he has it going on. The outside appearance is so unimportant, but to him it is everything. The outside appearance (the flesh) looks nice, but the inside (the soul) looks awful. I knew better. You have to be equally yoked.

We need a separation. In early February, I will make arrangements to move. I do not want to live like this anymore. I know I made a big mistake when I married a man that does not have the knowledge, love, or understanding of our God. God, let no Christian experience this. It is painful, and it hurts. We are unequally yoked, and I knew better, but what I wanted blinded me from what God's Word says. So I suffer, but by the grace of God I will not suffer much longer—not in that capacity. I will be single, and I pray to God that I will not be deceived again. I cannot imagine being divorced from him, though. I really love him, and it is sad that he does not love me in return. I want to be with someone who loves the Lord like I do and who has that God-like love for me and everyone else—someone who will accept me for me. I am only human, and I make mistakes as well. I will pray and ask God to show me what to do, and I know He will answer. I still have two months before I leave. This will be a hard thing to do, but it is best if things continue to be the same. God bless him, the kids, and the decisions I have to make. I am sorry. Jesus is Lord. Rkh .

December 8, 1998

I am watching *Beaches* with Bette Midler and Barbara Hershey—one of my favorite movies. I really get sentimental and cry when I watch this movie. I have friends that I have known for a long time, but never one that close like a sister. Right now, I am sad. I think of my sister and how hard those last days were realizing she wouldn't live. It leaves me sad and crying, and watching that movie did not help. I would have given anything for her to live—to be able to see her again and talk to her again. I know she went through a lot more than anyone will ever know. She was tired. She is resting now, and that gives me comfort. One night I dreamed that my youngest brother, who preceded her in death, walked up a flight of stairs and laid down beside my sister. I knew then she would not survive. I was just hoping.

I am tired of being mixed in this world with people who care no more about God than they do the dirt on the ground. If everyone knew Him, this world would be such a wonderful place. I am walking solely in God's strength these days. I have run out of my own strength. I have no more. It is hard. I really am at my wit's end. I don't know where to turn and whether to stay or go. I don't know what decision to make. Some moments I want to go, and then again I have moments I want to stay and try to work it out. Is it that I care too much about what other people will say? Can I accept that he will find someone else or go back to some one else? Why do I think of that? Why do I care that it will seem as though I failed in marriage, a two-time loser? But then I look around me, and there is so much sadness in this relationship, so many things to cry about, and so many things that have happened. So much hurt we have inflicted on each other. I have tried so hard. We have shared some precious moments, some moments that I will never forget. I will always love him.

It is different from before...maybe time will heal. That is what they say, right? I keep thinking of being alone, but that doesn't scare me at all. It sounds good—real good—but what would I do without him? What would he do without me? I am confused. Some days, I want to leave so badly—just walk right out the door and say good riddance and tell him all about himself with all his "blah, blah, blah" and tell him how he has broken my heart. But deep down inside, I believe that I have broken his heart too. I know there was a time when he really cared about me. I am not angry with him. I am just hurt and sorry, and in some ways I feel like we betrayed each other. We promised to love one another through thick and thin. But right now, he lives on the other side of the house, and that is that. He will not move out nor leave. He will just wait for me to leave. I am really considering going. It is more than just about me. It is other things too—like the children, my joy, and his joy. I know this is not a healthy environment for them, and I believe it is taking a toll on them. Their grades have suffered, and his attitude has changed toward them. He never had much to do with the kids. That is why I need to face facts. How can he love me and not at least care about the kids? How can I possibly think he loves me? But I do believe he does in his own stranger-than-life way. It is insane. Maybe I am hoping.

One day, I know that all things will be clearer. I am thinking about moving during spring break and finding some place close so that my son can go to the same school. So I have to stay in this area. What is the God thing to do? WWJD (What would Jesus do?) So much to lose, and so much to gain, and again I am walking in God's strength. I have no more. I love you, Jesus.

Afterthought: The movie *Beaches* depicts a true loss of a truly loved and cherished friend. "Did you ever know that you're my hero ... the wind beneath my wings?" That is probably just how I feel right now or worse, like losing something you really never thought you would lose. It is probably better if someone dies, because in death there is no choice. A divorce is harder. I think this is the hardest decision I have ever made, especially the most painful either way—hurt-stay-hurt-go-hurt. There is nothing else to do but wait until God answers... Rkh

December 9, 1998

Sermon notes: God probably is not like what we figure He is. What is God and who is God? God is omnipresent: everywhere, always here, never far, fills the void in all the earth, not limited to any special place or time. The Alpha and Omega, He is the author and finisher of our faith—El Shaddai, many-breasted one. God is all things to all people: dependent on no one else but Himself. "I am the God who can give life and sustain life—who made you, designed you, and will sustain you." Jehovah Rafa, helps us understand. God is omnipotent: God can do anything that will not violate His nature; God cannot lie; He has purity in character and cannot be improved; He is all powerful, unlimited, unrestricted. We are free moral agents with the option of making choices for our life. God will not force us to do anything. God knows everything and is able to know all things yet has given us a free will. We serve Him because we love Him and not because we had no choice. I made the choice; He did not force me to love Him. There is liberty in choosing and loving God. God does not honor rebellion. God will not share rebellion in His temple. We are predestined to go to heaven. The group you identify with has the mind of God and joins hearts and minds and souls with the body of Christ, you are heaven bound. God is omniscient: He knows everything, and from Him nothing is hidden. "As a man thinketh in his heart, so is he." In other words, what you think is what you become. Nothing goes unnoticed. We are not busybodies or know-it-alls. We should take care of our own business because we don't know it all like God. God is sovereign: ultimate ruler of the universe, and nothing can obstruct His will. Absolutely patient, but He will remove anything that tries to thwart His will. Immutable God: God's word cannot change, and God cannot change. Infinite God: No end, infinity never ends, on and on and on and on. God is an infinite God.

Where do we fit? Avoid foolish questions. We cannot explain God. We do not have to understand everything. We do not understand: cordless phones, electricity, fiber optics, etc., but we enjoy and utilize them to their fullest capacity. How can we be holy like God? God is not judging. He looks more at the base of intent. He is interested at the point of intent. God wants us to confess our sins with intention of abandoning sin. "Therefore, prepare your minds for action, practice self-control. Do not conform to evil as you did" (1 Peter 1). "Press on to a higher calling in hopes of a likeness of his image, minds transformed by the renewing of the Spirit. Spirit: Born again immediately. Soul: mind and will. Saved: if you do sin, you have an advocate, a process of sanctification. Each day, you get better and better. Strive to be holy like Jesus.

Reading in Proverbs: "The fool has said in his heart, 'there is no God.'" Don't judge anyone for goodness and/or badness. God is just, fair; every wrong is corrected. A loving God, compassionate. God is merciful, kind, patient—awesome. Thank you, Jesus! Rkh

December 11, 1998

Today was a hectic day. It is eight forty-four p.m., and I am just getting ready to settle down. Some days are better than others. I did not feel well this morning, but as the day went on I felt well enough to work and continue on. It is one of those blah days. My husband is still sleeping on the other side of the house. When will he come back? I left a message on his machine yesterday and today. Yesterday I told him, "Straighten up before my mother comes, buddy," and hung up. Today, I told him I was sick. He didn't call me. I guess he is still mad. I am too—just mad because I did not expect our marriage to be like this. I need that God kind of love. Only when God touches him will I get that from him. So I will wait. The Holy Spirit has been whispering in my ear, "Faith is the substance of things hoped for, the evidence of things not seen." I have been saying that a lot lately. I surely cannot change anything; I have to have faith in God. I'll just wait and see the salvation of God. God is looking for the kind of people who will trust Him regardless of their circumstances. These are the last days. God is good. Walk in his strength, not your own. If you try to walk in your own strength, you will fail...I love Jesus. Rkh

December 25, 1998

It is Christmas Day. We had a good Christmas. The kids are happy, I feel. I was glad to get them some of the things that they wanted. Although some things I guess will never change. Joe is gone because he is sponsoring a Christmas party tonight. He claimed that he needed to make the money. He stayed in that room practically all day, and I went on with the children and my grandbaby. I wish sometimes that he could really become a family man. He just does not care about things of that sort. It seems that everything is just about him. His actions are either self-serving, or he acts as if it just really does not matter. "Just another day to me." Sometimes I do not understand why I have to go through this. I took matters into my own hand without being honest and truthful to God, and now I have to suffer the consequences. So, I just pray that God will work this out for us. Joe's problems are spiritual and have nothing to do with me, and until I really realized that, it was almost driving me out of my own house and out of my mind. I was so close to leaving. I even put a deposit down on another place. But, I am still here.

The spirit of Christmas is to give, and I gave to everyone and feel good about it. He has his unopened presents, but I do not think he bought me anything. The best present I received anyway was the peaceful feeling that I have had throughout this holiday season. I know God is with me, and I know He is working all my troubles out. My flesh is really what is hurt, but my spirit is fine, because I know that it is not about me and my feelings. It is about a real relationship with God. I hope I can grow stronger in 1999, to where his attitude will not bother me at all. He has such a non-caring attitude toward me. He has no passion or consideration toward me. Our sex life is just that. We have not made love in a long, long time. This is not a complaint session, though. I am just getting my feelings out.

I love the Lord, and I know He hears my cry. God hears tears. I should have just dated Joe, but I had so much condemnation about sleeping with him without being married to him. It is not just him. It is obvious that I was not ready either. Now it is time to wait—to be patient and let God work. We have years ahead of us. We are young. We have a lot of years together, and I just have to be patient until God fixes my husband's heart and works with me too. It is one-o-six a.m., and I am alone. Christmas has come and gone, and Merry Christmas to all! God bless my family and my marriage. I love Jesus. He loves me. I know You are here always. You were there from the beginning, and You will be here until the end. Thank You for my health and my strength, for it all comes from You...Rkh

December 28, 1998

Dear God, I went to the Kirk Franklin, CeCe Winan, Trinity 5.7 concert. I had a good time. Now I am jotting down how I feel about the concert and how I feel right about now. I like praising Your name. I love praising Your name. You are more important than anything to me. Sometimes I know I probably act totally different, but God that is why I love You. You look deep down into my heart and know me better than I know myself. "For God so loved the world He gave his only begotten Son." That is awesome. That makes me want to give to show You how much I love You in return. I thank You for saving me and staying with me and never leaving me. You brought me this far, and by Your grace and mercy I am saved. I know that one day Your Son will come and rescue His children from all pain and suffering. I cannot wait for Jesus to come.

I am so tired of this world. People are so cruel, mean, insensitive, and selfish, and there are all those that do not know what love is all about. I am glad I know. I thank You for showing me. I thank You for guiding me. I thank You for all the things I went through to get to this point. I am at the point of no return. Sometimes I do not understand the whys, but I do know that You are always there, always loving, always caring, and always seeing me through. It is Your strength, and I am forever going to give You all the praise and glory. Forgive me, God for all my sins, and forgive my husband for all his because he doesn't know any better. As for me, I have no excuse because I do know better. Renew in me a clean heart and restore a right spirit in me. Thank You. I love You. Good night, Holy Spirit. Please wake me with a refreshed, clear, and peaceful mind, soul, and heart. Sometimes I get so disturbed by Joe's actions, but I am glad You are always there. You are my refuge and my very present help in times of storms. Love, Rkh

January 2, 1999

I thank You, God, for your grace and mercy to see me through another year. I love You, God. I love You for all the things You have been to me. You are everything to me, and You have been everything to me. If it was not for You and Your strength in me, I do not know where I would be. Lord, I pray that I grow closer to You and grow more and more like Jesus during this year. I know so many pray for more money or better jobs, and that is fine for them. But Lord, I pray for more of Your strength, for a peaceful New Year, and for Your strength and ability to deal with my situations. God, Your Word says you will not put more on us than we can bear. I believe Your every word. I pray in 1999 that You allow me the strength and courage to be peaceful, kind, loving, caring, longsuffering, patient, and obedient. If it was not for You, Lord, I know that my life would be more of a mess than I have already made of it. I pray that my family grows closer and stronger in Your love. I really started out tonight feeling frustrated—frustrated at the hands of someone who tries so hard to be the total opposite of a loving, kind human being. I do not know why he does that. If he only knew how sad I feel for him. I will love him whether he loves me or not. I will treat him like I know a child of God should treat anyone. I will pray constantly, and when I feel weak, I will look to God for his Help. Because I cannot do this, and I will mess it up.

Sometimes I want to tell him how ignorant he can be and how hateful and unkind he is, but God will deal with this. Thank You, God, for Your traveling mercies. Thank You, God, for allowing us to return home safely from our trip. Thank You for a new year, a new me, and a new life with You. I love You, and I look forward to worshipping on Sunday morning. I Love You! Love, Rkh

Afterthought: I really missed being in watch-night service, and God I know You know I would rather have Jesus than silver and gold. That is why I love my God. He knows me...me...me...me....

No Date

Dear God, I went to sleep when I got home. I turned on the small space heater, buried myself under the covers, and slept for about two hours. It was great. I cannot remember the last time I did that. Now I am eating chicken that I fried. Yummy! It feels good to just do what you want. I just cooked two pieces for me—one for tonight and one for work tomorrow. I knew everybody had already eaten. Today was back to the drawing board at work, but that is the norm. All the holidays, excitement, food, spending money, overeating, and gifts are gone, and I am glad they have gone. January is recovery month. Next year, I will start early. (I say that every year.)

Sunday was nice. Church was great. The message was about loving God with all your heart, mind, and soul. I went to Highland today. I really get fed when I go there. My other half went to Faith, of course. I hope and pray he grows there more this year. I hope the whole church grows and puts Jesus first and concentrates on the things of God, including a standard to live by. But in 1999, I know that I must grow. I know I must be taught. I will miss going to church with my husband, but I know that in 1999 I am going to chase after God, fall in love with God even more, and try hard to be obedient to my God. "Because God so loved the world that He gave his only begotten Son." This year, I will give—love, tithes, offerings, kindness, peace, and gentleness. With God's, help I can do this. I will always visit Faith, and maybe one day I will go back, but I think that it is time for me to go on. (Lord, help me if I am wrong.) I am in love with Jesus Christ. I cannot wait until Wednesday night.

I am also starting school again, getting my degree in Accounting. I know that with God's strength, I will be able to do this slow and easy. I can do all things with Christ Jesus who strengthens me. Thank You, Father, and I love You...Rkh

January 10, 1999

God! It is 1999! I remember Prince's song "Party Like It's 1999!" That seemed so long ago. Thank You, God, for all of those years you looked after me, carried me, and kept me safe from harm. I do not desire life without you. This world can have all the worldly things, but I would rather have Jesus than fortune or fame. You complete my life. You make me who I am and what I am today. Order my steps, Lord. I went to Highland today. The message was very inspiring. God, continue to guide me in the direction You would have me go. My desire is that my husband and I will one day worship You together. That does not mean he has to come to Highland or I have to go back to Faith. God, You know the future. Your will be done in this situation—Your will.

Help me to decrease so You can increase in me. Help me with my attitude with people, family, and friends. Help me to be like Jesus each day. Release the gifts I need to fulfill Your perfect will in my life. Help me read Your Word and receive the wisdom and knowledge of Your words. Help me hide Your Word in my heart. Help me to be a light at home, at work, and everywhere I go in 1999 and forever. I need You, Lord. My husband said he was going to seminary school. I do not know where that is going, but Lord, Your will be done in his life also.

God bless Michelle and her entire family, Joyce and her family, Celia's, Marie's, James' and the whole Maintenance Division at my job. God bless my family in North Carolina and especially my son Chad (as a young adult). Lord, please help him and keep him safe from harm. I plead the blood of Jesus over his life, and Lord, help him make wise decisions for himself. I pray a special blessing for all my children and all the children in the world. God bless this world. We definitely need You. Come, Lord. Even now, Lord, come. Glory to God! Hallelujah, the King is coming. Every knee shall bow and every tongue shall confess that Jesus is Lord. Work tomorrow, and school starts. Thank You, Lord, for making a way for me to go back to school. You are so worthy. You are so good. Taste and see the goodness of the Lord. Love, Rkh

January 26, 1999

Dear Lord, I am sitting here tonight. I have watched my favorite thing to watch on television besides TBN. This lady and her boyfriend were agreeing to see other people and see if they would have a *Change of Heart* (the show). She was practicing celibacy, and they had never slept together. I thought that was very exceptional. She went out with someone more mature and spiritual like herself. He with someone who loved to party and was ready for anything. After the hot date, the man wanted to stay with his current girlfriend and did not have a change of heart. But she changed her mind and decided to start dating her blind date that shared her maturity, had a child himself, and also practiced celibacy. I thought that was so special. She was very beautiful and he was very handsome.

I thought about how I slept with Joe in one month—three weeks, to be exact. I can remember the time when I could just think of him and I would want to be with him. That is gone, it seems. We hardly ever have sex. And romance? Out of the picture these days. Make love? Ha! I remember when it was great. He was great, and I knew he loved me. Or I thought so anyway. He thinks that is cute too. I think it is awful. I am not amused by it in the least. I remember what he told me one night when he said, "Woman, I love you so much, you just do not know." I knew that I would always love him, and I knew that no matter what happened between us, he would always be my dream earthly husband, and I thought how can I ever leave? So, I stay married. He does not treat me lovingly. I find that most of the time, I am the one making this work and keeping the peace.

I dislike the way he talks about my children or the lack thereof. I can hardly find the time to feel romantic toward him anymore. That is so sad, because most of the time, it is some little nasty remark or something he has said to me or about one of my children. The children just aggravate him anyway. They really do not have to do anything. Teenagers are going to be teenagers regardless. He doesn't understand that. That is why I am going to try to just help them grow up in a happy environment while they are here. I just want them to know that I do care. I love kids, and I always have. It is hard trying to maintain a stable environment when most of the time he is in a bad mood with me, and he hardly ever shows any emotion. Especially when bills are behind and we do not have money and have to wait for payday. It is in God's hands. You know, this man goes to church and says he is a Christian. He has a radio ministry, gives to the church considerably, and sings in the choir. He is definitely handsome in appearance, but something on the inside is not right.

Does anyone know what God has done? Does anyone know the God I serve? Does anyone know that God's will for us is that we be like Jesus? Do I really know myself? Lord, I am trying so hard. Why don't they know? I know that I am not perfect, but I do not harbor hate, wrath, jealousy, dislike, and strife in my heart. Where is the change? Change me, Lord. I am not judging, but God's Word says, "Judge by the fruit they bear." What kind of fruit am I bearing? If it is not good fruit, then today, tonight, I ask the Holy Spirit in Jesus' name to change me inside out—inside out.

Something on the inside working on the outside. Work on the inside of me, Lord Jesus. Renew in me a clean heart and a right spirit. I am sorry, Father, for the argument Saturday at work. I should not have gotten so angry. That is not good fruit. I must apologize to everyone. Lord, help me be stronger and committed to You and change the things I can and the wisdom to know to leave the things I cannot change alone.

Afterthought: Paul said, "I learned to be content in all things..." Rkh.

January 28, 1999

Dear God, what a day and night. I have been driving back and forth since seven-thirty. Poor car and poor me! I am tired, so tired. Well, home life is the same. You know, my husband continues to sleep in the bedroom on the other side of the house. Who would have gotten remarried for that? I do not know why he does that—whether it's his upbringing, social problems, or psychological problems. God, I am trying to work on me. I cannot do it without You. You are the only one who really cares about me. You are always there to pick me up and to whisper in my ear and wipe away my tears. You were always there, even before I even knew You, preparing me for such a time as this.

When I was blind, You were my eyes. When I was in pain, suffering emotionally, physically, and spiritually, You were there. You are everything to me, Lord God, and I dedicate my life to You. Please help me be a light and to decrease so that You can increase in me. Help me keep myself positive and to forgive others just as You have forgiven me. Help me to grow in discernment, love, peace, kindness, gentleness, longsuffering, and patience. I am tired of hurting, God. Shield me from this ugly marriage. Help me accept how things are right now. Carry me through these times, as I am a victim of others' disbelief and lack of faith. You are so good. Why can't they see? Woe is me! But through it all, I feel Your comfort, Your peace, and Your stronghold holding me up when I want to just fall to the ground. I never thought my marriage would be this way. I thought we cared too much for each other.

But business is business. We have to live, to keep a roof over our heads, and unfortunately right now that is just about all it is. Without two standing together loving God, how can a home be a home, a father be a father, a stepfather love enough and show he cares, a husband love his wife, and a wife love her husband? Without two people believing, living, and trusting in Jesus, it will not happen. God, You promised me in Your Word that You would give me the desires of my heart. Are my desires wrong for me? Will they lead me astray from You? Will they cause me to die and go to hell? If so, God, then let Your will be done in my life and send Your Son to rescue all of us who believe and love You. Rkh

Afterthought: Money will not buy happiness or anyone's love. You have to be the object of their affection like we are to God. I guess that is the way it will always be. Thank You, God, for sustaining me, because if it weren't for You, I would not make it.

February 1, 1999

A new month. Here we go again. Lately, always an attitude. I see his face—always so tight, so hard and never soft and warm, never inviting. It is so different from the beginning. The devil is so busy and always stirring up evil, and that is why I will never turn around. Never. He is just out to kill, steal, and destroy. But, I know that I have the victory. It is already done. Jesus died! He hung his head and He died. Just to know that no matter who may leave, Jesus will never leave. And if I fall, He will pick me up again and again. That is how awesome Jesus is. He continues to whisper in my ear, "Rkh, do not weep," and I weep because of His goodness—not because of my circumstances, but because I know that Jesus will work it out by and by. There is a God that reigns high and that looks low and brings victory to His children. No matter how long it takes or how He works it out, I will lift my head and know it was or is for my good.

I was so cold when I got home from work. I thought things were a little better, but as soon as I saw him, I asked him to hold me because I was shivering. He said, "Put your coat on." I had my coat on already. So I just went into my room (remember, he sleeps on the other side of the house most of the time) and got under the covers and called on the name of Jesus. I stopped instantly. I am not shivering any longer. Hallelujah! He is always there. The Lord never changes. I am the apple of His eye. Every situation is already won. Life or death, victory. No human can ever give that. He said, "Come lay down your burdens, and I will give you rest " (peace, joy, happiness, patience, longsuffering, kindness, gentleness, meekness, love etc.). Thank You, Lord, for teaching me how to love and trust in You. If we all knew, we would all be in heaven. Rkh

Afterthought: Thank You for carrying me another day. Without You, I am nothing. Carnal eyes cannot and are not capable of seeing and understanding spiritual things. Until the blinders are lifted, "there is a way that seems right to a man, but the road leads to destruction." This is God's blessed Word!

After afterthought: "Pick up My yoke. It is easy; try Me and see. I am God. I am not mocked! I am God; I am not a man that I shall lie or the son of man that I shall repent."

February 4, 1999

I really felt vulnerable today. I felt like starting up something. But, I prayed about it. I went into my closet and I talked to God about it. I wanted some attention; after all, I am his wife. But, I don't want any attention unless it is positive attention. I am not holding my breath waiting for it either. I feel like just leaving this troubled man behind. He has the problem, whatever it is. Me, her, them, and whoever, I am tired. I did tell him not to push me (physically), but when I tried to show him my autographed photo, he just pushed me aside like "You are not worth the time of day to me. Neither is anything you have, will ever have, or will ever attempt to have. It and you are the last thing on my mind." I told him not to push me and that he had already pushed me too far. And then I left, like he cared. I feel like he played a really bad dirty joke on me. It is as though no matter how hard you try, you just cannot shake the bad feeling. Why did he marry me? God, someday I hope this will be answered. I want to know the truth. It is obvious that whatever love, like, interest, or use he had for me has since died. We have not kissed in probably three months. He has not said he loves me in three months. Who does he think he is that he can just treat people like they do not matter? Control is the name of that game. It is like some kind of obligation or some kind of "I will show you" directed at his ex-girlfriend.

I am on the sidelines just waiting, just watching, hoping to participate. Did I deserve this for jumping in so quickly? My friends told me not to, but I really thought we loved each other. I never dreamed it would be this way! But reality is just that—reality! I know if there is ever a next time, I will date for years and try to be celibate. I am just holding on by a thread. I love You, Jesus. Rkh .

February 6, 1999

Here I sit in this building that I have become so familiar with. I don't come here enough. This is a place of refuge for me. It is so peaceful here—a place to worship, think, and read, and in this instance, write. I do not know if I am writing what I should: my intentions were not to bash anyone. But to just write down some thoughts and things that are on my mind and the things that are happening in my life. I am at Highland in the newly erected praying tower—the tower erected for a community. Everyone is invited to come, and it stands tall for all to see. I love this place, and again I do not come as often as I should. Last night was a night. We had sex, made love, whatever—it was nice just to have him touch me. It had been at least three weeks maybe. I cannot keep up. But, he is the only one I have to make love to and be right in the eyes of God. I do not desire to be with anyone else. I will just become celibate if we get a divorce. Nevertheless, we are right back to that division thing, as if last night did not happen. I would like to think that making love is like something magical that lingers around for days. I loved you and you loved me, and we came together to forgive and forget the entire world and the wrong we have done to each other. Let's start anew. The magic is gone again, only lasting until the reality of it all kicks in again. I get the feeling that my husband does not want to be bothered most of the time. The sad thing about it is that I am getting used to being treated like that.

Lately, he is always angry with me or with one of the children about something. I do believe that I should have remained single. That is awful to say, I know, but I ask for God's forgiveness. I do not want to leave because I believe God will fix my marriage one day. It is so hard to be patient when the circumstances look so different from what you believe. I cannot give up; it is something in me that will not allow me to walk away. I only pray that whatever it is inside me that gives me the strength and courage to hang in there is of wisdom, knowledge, and of God. I hope that it isn't any type of dysfunctional dependency, weakness, ignorance, or fear. I have to keep my focus on my children and not let this hinder me from fulfilling my duties as a parent. I am their mother, and they look for me to take care of them. That is my honor and my duty as a parent. They are all wonderful kids, and I adore them. They are a tad bit irritating at times, but I know that is just because they are children—you know the usual stuff: not keeping his room clean, throwing paper towels everywhere but in the trash can, leaving pop cans in their room, etc. That is nothing to me. Irritating, yes, but I know it is just kid stuff. I am sure we all did irritating things to our parents when we were young. I know I did. I have come to the conclusion when they leave, my husband will still be angry about something. He is just an angry person, and he needs Jesus to heal his angry heart. He needs Jesus to come into his life and make him the man he should be to me and to the kids and to the world. A real man loves Jesus and tries to do the things he knows Jesus would be pleased about. But instead, it is always anger, selfishness, and unhappiness, just like the devil would have it. Well, I should not say always. Ultimately, somehow it always comes right back to that. I just do the best that I can under the circumstances. I cannot change these circumstances, and if I could, it would change this moment. Nor can I change a heart or mind. Only God can.

Lord, I pray, let something touch his heart and soften it toward You. Let the Holy Spirit come into his life so boldly, so strongly that he cannot deny the power of You. Fix his mind on You, Lord God, and change his ways. Until You do this, I know that this relationship will not change. No matter how much we gain, we lose each other without You. Lord, please do not let that happen because we both need You. Not just me; he needs You too. We need You together. When, God? When? I love you, God, and I trust You. Even though I hurt because of marital issues, one day I will write about how You fixed it. I know I will. "Trust and believe," You say; I do. Until then, my Lord, keep me close to Your bosom and comfort me. I am Your child. Nobody can ever take that away. I can always hide in You and be comforted by You and the Holy Spirit. So as the wind blows and toss me to and fro, I will hang on to the anchor that will never let me go. Thank You, Lord, for peace that surpasses all understanding. Rkh

Afterthought: WWJD? He would keep on His journey and live right

72

and do what God would have Him to do. That is what He did in spite of the treatment, name calling, abuse, the lies, and the painful death He endured. He stood (lived) for God, and He died for us. Glory! Hallelujah! Jesus is Lord!

February 27, 1999

I cannot believe it has been that long since I have written in my book, since February 6, 1999. Time flies. Jesus will come one day, and that will be the best time ever. That will be a hallelujah, shouting, and singing, stomping, and clapping good time. Well, until then we just press on...press on in spite of the obstacles in the way. I am getting older, and I know I need to stop saying that. I am glad to have lived to see this age. I have one brother who died at twenty-seven years old and one sister who died at thirty-four years old. I am truly blessed to be here today. I thank God for keeping me. The Trinity—the Father, the Son, and the Holy Ghost; they are awesome. I am so glad to be a believer today. I am glad to know the Lord today. I am glad to know that one day I will be with Jesus.

I am not going to write long tonight. I am trying to study for an algebra class—a test on Monday. My mate is at McLean's (I really do not like him to go there), but he said he was going to make a few extra dollars. Somehow, I think that is like punishment for me because he feels I did not do what he wanted me to do. So the kids are sleeping peacefully, and I am sleepy myself. I have been cleaning most of the day after I finally got up out of the bed. Lord, thank You for the rest. I was reading my notes from February 6, 1999, and I can already see You working meticulously in my life; since then I have seen a lot of things happening. I marvel at Your wonder, Your splendor, Your grace, Your mercy, and Your excellence. God, help me be humble. Continue the work that unfolds daily before my eyes. I love You, Father. Church tomorrow. I am excited. Rkh

Afterthought: Glory hallelujah, the reason why I sing!

February 28, 1999

I just wanted to briefly write tonight. Today's service was very good. Oh, to be truly fed. I thought of my sister, and I always like thinking of her, although it was a very sad ending. I know that she is okay. She is happy and

73

not suffering emotionally and physically any longer. Hallelujah. You spoke those very words to me when I was grieving. I just could not understand why she had to unexpectedly die of cancer at such a young age—why she had to leave two small children behind who needed her. But, Lord, I thank You for Your words: "She is in a better place than you are." At that moment the healing process began, and I understood that I needed to grieve and believe that You are God and in control of everything. She had suffered enough. If it had not been for You, Lord, I would not have made it through that period. Lord, You are a God that does not make mistakes. Your love is unconditional. Please help me to love others the same way You love us and to communicate that love to everyone. I love You, God, with all my heart and soul, and I thank You, Lord, for being patient with me. I love my life with You. I miss my baby sister so much, but I know that You know what is best. I know she is in heaven, smiling, and free of any sickness or disease. As my daughter always said, even as a child, "When Auntie smiles, her eyes smile too." Rkh

April 2, 1999

I have not written anything since February 28, 1999—in over a month. Things now are not as I would like them to be, but I know that God knows best and is in control of my life. "All things work together for the good for those who are the called according to his purpose." My highlight is the church I attend. I am really thankful for the Holy Spirit and the Word that is "sharper than a two-edged sword." (Ouch! Watch out, or it will cut you!) There is so much that is going on in that church. I mean, God is doing awesome wonders. I cannot imagine why my spouse will not even visit. That is my only regret for changing churches. My husband still goes to Faith. I miss him so much beside me during service. I look at the other couples, and I long for him to be with me worshipping and loving God in all spirit and all truth. God is molding me for preparation to live with him in heaven. You know, I really believe that with all my heart. I thank God that He touched me. So many just have a knowledge or a yearning or a something (a "form of godliness" that the Bible speaks about) but forsake all the power, all the glory, and all the supernatural splendor of a God who gave His Son for us when we did not deserve that. Thank You, Lord, for grace and mercy.

Lord, there are so many reasons to give up in life—Kosovo, death, murder, hunger, anger, gossiping, backbiting, mistreatment, hurt, selfishness, greed, envy, covetousness, adultery—I could go on and on. Even now, my husband and I are not speaking. He is sleeping in what he calls "his room" again. He will not even sleep with me. I keep thinking, "What did I do that was so bad that he cannot even sleep with me for six days straight?" Then I think of all the reasons why I should not sleep with him, and it is sort of funny. I slept in that bed even if I had to cry myself to sleep.

Nothing is ever as bad as it seems, especially not when you know the Lord Almighty. Sometimes I feel, but then, who cares about feelings? Satan plays with emotions and feelings. Still, in my mind I feel like I am the one who got cheated because I wanted a godly man—a man that loved God. Not a perfect man, but a man who knew that God and commitment are first, not a job or a "hobby" you had before you knew God. Not the attitude of "I have been playing golf all my life, and I am going to play golf until I die." What are you saying? That if it means giving up something or curtailing something to have a relationship with God, you just will not do it? Is it something you want to hold on to because you really do not want to give up anything for God, even though you know He gave up His only Son for you? Are you a believer, or do you just believe in what you want to believe in and the parts you want to believe in? Why go to church, I ask, if you do not believe or are not willing to change? Do you just want the blessings of God but not to do what God says?

Sometimes I watch my husband flipping through the channels, and it is like once he gets to the Christian channel, a rebellious spirit comes upon him, and he does not even seem interested in what "thus said the Lord." There is just the look of defiance on his face that I see—coldness toward the Word of God. As much as this has happened, he has never once stopped to listen to a sermon by anyone, black or white, man or woman. In four years, I have seen him do this time after time. When will he stop? Will he ever stop running, or will I live in his misery until Jesus comes back? I will if I have to, because I knew what the Bible said. "Ye must be equally yoked." I knew, but I had to have it *my* way. I do not feel like my husband cheated me, for I know I cheated myself. But hallelujah, I believe in a just God who said, "I will give you the desires of your heart." So I know one day, we will be joined together in the Lord, worshipping God in spirit and in truth. I believe that because I serve a risen Savior who gave His life for a friend.

Another thing is that I have been taught and shown the true meaning of love, and love does not give up, is not unkind, is patient, etc. The one thing is, I love him with all my heart, even though I know that he has faults. I know that I am not an angel. I do so many things wrong and have made so many mistakes in my life. I am not judgmental; I cannot call the kettle black. But the one difference I see is that I know my faults and weaknesses and ultimately, I know I need God in my life. God, bless my husband and me. We both need You. I need You every second, every minute of the day, and I know this. Rkh

No Date

Dear God, I thank you for today. I know that You are real, that You love me, and that You are working things out for me. All I need to do is just be still and trust and believe in You that "all things will work together for my good" because I am the "called according to your purpose." I will keep You as my focus when things around me seem hopeless. I will have hope, peace, joy, and You to talk to. I am so thankful that I have a God to talk to. I know You will comfort me. You have so many times before. That makes me strong. I love You, and nothing will change that. My tears are for him because I know how much I love him. I hope he knows. But I certainly know that he does not know how much you love him. That is so sad to me. It is sad that I do not know where my husband is. I do not know if he is hurting or not. I saw his face twice this week. He looked sad. He looked like he was very tired and had not slept in days. I saw him for only a second each time. I want so much for us. I want both of us to know You. I want us to be together forever until You come again or take one of us home. Lord, bless my husband and my marriage. I know You will. Rkh

Afterthought: Bless all the children!

April 5, 1999

Dear God, I believe I can fly! Thank you, God. I could not be more pleased with the D in algebra. God, I am glad it is over. Whew! I know that You and You alone allowed me to pass. So many times I gave up. I quit studying and just said, "I will take it over." But, now I do not have to, and I will gracefully accept my Academy Award for "A D in Algebra, Best Supporting Actor, Jesus Christ!" Hallelujah! Thanks to You, Jesus, and a friend who is always there when I need him—the friend that you placed in my life a long time ago who has been like a brother to me. Thank God for true friends. I love You, Lord, and I am still holding on. Waiting, waiting patiently for You to intervene in all my situations. I love You so much, and I thank You for sending Your Son to die on the cross for me. That's Love! Rkh

Afterthought: "For God so loved the world, He gave…"

April 10, 1999

Dear God, please forgive me for all my sins. Each day, it seems I am less worthy to be called Your child. But, yet and still I am Your child no matter what I do. I cannot change that one truth. We are all Your children. How great is that? How great is Thy faithfulness? You "saved a wretch like me." Sometimes life gets so tough, and I feel like giving up, but I know that You will not give up on me. I do not know what I want to give up on: myself, school, or life, but God is the one thing I do believe in. I certainly do not believe in me and my abilities or anything in this world. I know He will give me the strength to continue on. "Keep your eyes on the prize," He whispers in my ear.

I have lived a long time and have endured a lot of things. I should see some signs of maturity and spiritual development. Some days I think I am progressing right along, and then other days I feel like I have taken two steps backward. Lord willing, I will see many more days that I have made progress. I hope Jesus comes soon. I long to be with my Father—with the only real father that I have ever known—and I am homesick. Sometimes I just feel so sad because the world still continues to deny Jesus, to turn away from Jesus, and still does not believe or care to believe. The Bible says, "Narrow is the road." Everyday, more and more as I live, I know that to be true. People do not really know the Lord, and that is just not a judgment call, for who am I to judge? Especially someone like me. What makes me so different? Someone is looking at me probably saying the same thing, especially when I am acting or carrying myself in a less than godly manner or when I definitely am not acting with godly character, and they are clearly seeing my faults. Lord, please help me get my attitude together. Where did such an attitude come from? Help me to serve You in spirit and in truth.

God, I am unworthy. I still have a bad attitude and an ugly disposition sometimes. Please change me. I cannot do it myself. I need You to do that for me. I need Your strength, guidance, and direction. Please, Lord, help me start tonight right now. For all the reasons to be sad, deep down inside I still feel peace. God, you know I love you very much. Please bless my marriage; please bless the children. Help me go on and grow closer to You and to continue to worship you in spirit and in truth. Thank You, Lord, for everything You have done for me. I love you. Rkh .

Afterthought: God, bless my husband and his Christian walk.

April 11, 1999

Well, in two days, I will be another year older and hopefully another year wiser. Amazing. Thank You, Lord. I am not doing anything special for my birthday. I wanted a party, but I guess after so much strife and confusion between me and my spouse, I did not really feel like celebrating anyway. I will be in class after work, and that will be just fine with me. I really just feel like it is just another day, just the day I was born. The most important day is the day I was born again—February 13, 1992.

I want no part of the worldly things most people are caught up in. Thanks solely to God. I was there once, and I have tasted both sides. Today was an interesting day. Just when I thought nothing could beat some of the things that already happened, boom! It is really amazing the things I have gone through in the last four or five years. I know if I did not know the Lord, I would not be with anyone at this time. I would get a divorce immediately and move on. I am not even scared of moving on either. I just know that I vowed before God to be committed to this union and will just have to suffer until God changes the situation. There will be a change some day. Just as Jesus suffered at the hands of many, I will endure because I know God will step in. Either way, God's will be done in my life. The song I am listening to now is "Stand." I have prayed and cried, prayed and cried. I know God will step in. He came in complaining, moaning, and groaning about this and that. We kind of got into a spray can altercation, and he twisted my wrist relatively hard—enough for me to feel it anyway. I was trying to clean up, and he was just getting home from work. I asked him why he did not just stay at work if this is the way he was going to act. He was complaining about who had his movies, where his spade was, where was the VCR he bought and so forth and so on. He really was aggravating me. I just said, "You have lost your mind." Sometimes I wonder who he thinks he is or, better still, who does he think I am? (My attitude showing up.) That is definitely why we butt heads most of the time. I do not even warrant a "Hello. How was your day?" or a kiss. So I just said, "Okay, whatever." He left to go to the store to get milk and came back home with the same attitude and had the nerve to make a rude comment. No "Thanks for making dinner" or "I appreciate it" or "I know I was wrong"—nothing. I cleaned the entire house out of frustration. If I had not, it would look like that room back there where he often sleeps and keeps his stuff. It is filthy. He is living in filth, unacceptable, and children living in filth, even more unacceptable. He just retreated to that room and closed the door. I had to leave, so I told him dinner was ready and I left with the kids.

That is the sign of a very self-absorbed individual. God, what was I thinking? He is so selfish. The things he does. He keeps the computer in his room and keeps the door locked so I cannot use the computer unless he allows me to when we are on good terms. I really was enjoying the Internet, and all of a sudden one day he got angry and locked it in his other room. He got angry because I hung up his clothes and folded some other clothes he had all over the chair that had been there for weeks. I did it because I needed the space for my work. He then accused me of messing with his stuff and locked the door after throwing my work and purse out of the room. The door has been locked ever since. Most people would appreciate things like that and would say, "Thanks," or something, but not him. I like a clean house and I do not mind cleaning, cooking, doing yard work, etc. I have a good job with good benefits, and I love the Lord. I go to school and to church, and mainly that is it. Most of the time I am happy in the Lord. Most people would appreciate someone like me, but it seems he detests me and everything associated with me. That is so weird, so abnormal. Anyway, we went to a marriage counselor once before, and she asked him a series of questions about what his issues were with me, and he could not identify any. She asked questions like, "Does she keep a clean house? Does she take care of the children? Does she cook?" etc. He had no complaints, but he did tell her that if he found someone else, he would leave (or something like that). She summed him up in a nutshell: She said, her words exactly, "You have a spiritual problem." He did not like that, so we never went back. She called me the next day to see if I was okay because some of the things he said were harsh. I guess she thought I was devastated and hurt, and she was concerned. I appreciated that, but I was not devastated. I was downright embarrassed. We never spoke again after that.

There is something very wrong with this picture. I was listening to the radio, and he came in and turned the TV up so loud that I could not hear the radio. I guess it is because it is his TV. Anyway, well, God, it is in Your hands. You know what I go through. It is difficult because I do not know how to handle all this strife and anger. Most of the time, I definitely react wrong. It is hard to ignore, and the more I ignore it or accept it, the worst it gets. But God, I know I have already said more than I should. It sounds like a complaint session. I have actually said too much to my spouse in anger as well. I know he is angry with me now. I just gave him a solid reason to be nasty and mean. He probably feels okay about himself right about now. Now it is just endure, endure, hold on, hold on. God will step in, and I know He will see me through this. I trust and believe in God. Lord, give me the strength to keep holding on even when my heart is so disappointed. WWJD? Rkh

Afterthought: "Keep your eyes on the prize… keep your eyes on the prize… eyes on the prize… eyes on the prize."

April 15, 1999

Dear God, my birthday came and went, and no one really acknowledged it. I was alone as far as humans are concerned, but God was with me all day. I felt really good and enjoyed taking myself to lunch and eating steak even though Outback Steakhouse did not open until five p.m., so I had to go somewhere else. I had a class at six. I did not tell anyone it was my birthday. But when I went to the bank, the teller noticed and said, "Happy birthday." That was so nice of her. Joe did not even talk to me all day or night and did not acknowledge my birthday at all. But it was nice, and I felt like I had a secret between God and me all day long. No one knew but us. No one cared but us. My spirits were up, and I have come to the conclusion that I am going to stop and smell the roses! I am going to enjoy the rest of my life, whatever time I have left. Thank you, Lord, even though I would have loved to get flowers, dinner and a gift; God came through and gave me the peace that surpassed my own understanding. Thank You, Jesus—alone in His presence.

I also heard some disturbing news today. One nineteen-year-old female was shot and killed yesterday. I knew her when she was fifteen years old. She worked with us as a summer hire some years back. I really had not thought about her much along the years, but she did call once, and on another occasion I saw her name in the paper where she had given birth to another baby. That made two children for her at such a young age. Well, at age nineteen with three children, her boyfriend shot her to death. She is dead at nineteen years old. Sometimes I wonder if I ever told her about God, to go to church, or if I helped her in any way. I hope that I was never mean or rude or treated her badly. No one knew that she was going through such a rough time in her young life. I cannot remember, but I hope we were all nice to her and made a difference in her life during all those days she worked with us. She really was just a child, and at fifteen had a son and soon after another. I remember her saying that her and her mother did not get along, and she was staying with her sister at that time. She could sing so beautifully. I remember that well. Now, she is dead. That really hurt my heart when I heard that. Lord, I can only hope that she is singing love songs to You.

I love You, God, and maybe this sounds crazy. Maybe some will not understand (if anyone ever get the opportunity to read this). Celebrate my birthday if you want, but when I die, celebrate my death for sure, because I will be with my Lord and Savior Jesus Christ celebrating! Hallelujah! Glory to God! Amen! Rkh.

Afterthought: "Be still and know that I am God. Keep your eyes on the prize!"

April 16, 1999

Dear God, I love You. You are always with me, and I thank You every second for Your grace and Your mercy, because I know that I am not even worthy of it. In spite of myself, You love me anyway. That is the kind of love I want to have and to give. It is called "agape love." Lord, I am anticipating Your return; whether it is the year 2000 or 3000, I know You will come in all Your glory. Thank You, Lord, for loving me and for the wonderful care You give me. Thank You for watching over me. Help me be a light in this dark world. Help me decrease, Lord, so that You may increase in me. Help me in all areas in my life. Home first—help me be a light for my family first and then, Lord, to others. Help me spread the gospel and not only tell of Your goodness, but let my life shine so brightly that when I tell my testimony, lives will have to change, people will have to change, and circumstances will have to change. Let there be change in all the earth! My tears are for You, and my longing is to have a world full of Christians that love You and Your Son. "How can they hear without a preacher?" We all have that responsibility, so we must somehow find ways to tell those we come in contact with in our families, our workplaces, and those we meet along the way. Please, Lord, help me be a better witness to win souls for You. Love, Your daughter, Rkh

Afterthought: You are my Father. Renew in me a clean heart and a right spirit. Use me.

May 23, 1999

Dear God, thank You for sending me to Highland. I joined the church, and I am really happy I did. Lord, it has been over a month since I have written. You know what has been happening. At this time, my spouse is sleeping in the other room again (his room, shall I say). Sometimes I just wish I had stayed single. Lord, You know how much I struggled with being single too. Is life always a struggle? I know I am here with him through thick and thin. I know You will open his eyes one day. I must trust and believe in that. (When God? When?) You told me You would, and I believe You will. So with that I will not drag on and on about that situation. I would love to give that situation totally to You. But sometimes I am afraid. I am frightened, and I keep thinking that there is something I can do.

I love You, Lord, and I know You will be with me until the end. The end—it is a long, narrow, hard, hilly, winding road that leads to the end, but at the end there will be peace, joy, happiness, and no more crying. I know You are working a wondrous work in me. I can feel myself letting go and letting you. I no longer want to be cruel, angry, and mean, to backbite or to hurt anyone. I find myself praying for everyone, even those that do not treat me well or spitefully use me. Lord, I am Your servant.

Another issue on my mind: My oldest son got in trouble for drugs, for illegal substance and possession of an illegal substance. It is a misdemeanor with a fine of $290. When I heard about that, my heart broke. I cried and cried and cried—not for the money, not for his having to stay in jail a couple of nights, but for his future. At one point, I howled like a hurt animal as I aimlessly drove around. I heard the sound of pain today. I heard the sound of pain when my mother cried each morning as she awoke to realize that her son was gone forever, like the cry of a hurt animal, a pain so deep, so certain, and so sure. But I had never heard the pain of my own cry. I heard the sound of pain today, and as unfamiliar as it was, I listened carefully and realized that the sound was coming up from my very own belly, and I could not control it. I could not stop, but I listened intently. It was strange that I was aware of the sound of my pain and at the same time so hurt that I could not control my cry. It was frightening, almost like going over the deep end and watching yourself submit to it. I cried for fifteen minutes straight, I think. All I can remember is that I listened and knew that that was the deepest pain I had ever felt, and at the same time I knew that only God could heal a pain like that. I surrendered to Him and not to the pain, and He kept me, and I grew from that pain. I went on to make some of the hardest decisions I had ever had to make. I went on afraid, hurt, and unsure, but I grew. I grew closer to God and gained a better understanding of myself and my God. The understanding I grew to know is that in this life, we shall all have pain, and it is ultimately for the perfecting of the saints! My spouse never knew how much that hurt my heart, nor did he care. But I knew God cared enough to sustain me again. I know He brought me back from a point of no return. What if I had not known Him? I am still praising God because I know that God was there to comfort me and carry me when I was helpless. He let me know that it was not the end of the world, even though it felt like it. I praised God anyway. That is something I have learned along the way. I know that He is real, and it is in His strength that I move and breath. My strength ran out years ago. God gave me the strength to endure. I pray for my son who is here with me now for a while. He will be going to take his physical for the Marines on June 14. I pray he will leave those drugs alone. That is in God's hands now. God worked it out so I did not have to pay the money for my son's fine. My son had the money, which he had earned working in Tennessee. Glory, hallelujah! God knows I did not have the money to spare. He is still able to go into the Marines. He had already passed everything except the physical. Lord God, bless him and help him know You and open his eyes to You and Your love. Keep him safe from all harm.

Also, lest I forget, bless my youngest son who might have to go to summer school. I am praying to God that a miracle happens and he will not have to go. The cost for summer school is $200 a class. I do not have $200. I know my God, and He is "able to do exceedingly, abundantly above all that we could ever ask." Thank You, God, for Your mercy and Your grace. "For God so loved the world that He gave"....Rkh

Afterthought: There are so many reasons to be discouraged and only one reason not to be—God! Hallelujah! Rkh.

May 28, 1999

Dear God, today was a hard day. I am glad that it is over. Things are not going like I want them to go, but You are the conductor. I know that You know what is best for me. You know what I need. The pain that I am going through right now is for my own good. So many things have happened with my oldest son, with my youngest son, and with my spouse. It is enough to make anyone cry. But I know, Lord, that you are there; I know that this too will pass. It is hard to keep focused and think positively and maintain a spiritual focus, but that is what You called us to do, even in the hard, trying times. Lord, You are looking for true Christians, for Christians who stand the test of times, who honor and obey You regardless of circumstances. Lord, please give me the courage to continue to do the things I know You have called me to do. Lord, I know that I have so much to do. Holy Spirit, guide me every step of the way. Help me birth the vision. God,

You know the vision, I know the vision, and I need your guidance.

Tonight I saw Suzanne Taylor. What an inspiration for You she is! Thank You for allowing me to see her. She is in touch with You. Lord, when I speak, let it be unto You, glorifying You, introducing You to nonbelievers and those who are not quite sure of what it is they need to do. I need to make that "change." Where do I begin? Is it time? Lead me, Father, lover of my soul. I love You, Father. I love You, Jesus. I love You, Holy Spirit. Please renew in me a clean heart and a right spirit. Love, Your child, Rkh

May 31, 1999

Dear God, today is Memorial Day—a holiday, I am just laying in the bed thinking, thinking, thinking, reflecting. The one thing I know for sure is that You are always with me, no matter what is going on. I still have peace and joy, and that is amazing, almost inconceivable. It is amazing, and I know that must be why the song "Amazing Grace" has been so popular for the saved; because Your grace and mercy is awesome, and You love us and have great compassion for us in spite of who we are. Lord, thank You for the Holy Spirit who lives within me. Even when I want to fall apart, the Holy Spirit will not let me. You will not let me. Even when I am disappointed, You still remain the strength, the force that binds me. There was a time when I dwelled on my hurt, but over the years I know better. I've learned that dwelling on hurt, disappointment, and mistakes will leave you bitter and angry. Bitterness and anger can cause you to lose touch with what is important in life. It will control you, and then Satan will have a field day with your mind and emotions. I mean, he will literally destroy us and our relationships if we allow him. But I know a God that sits high and looks low, who sent His only Son so that we may have life and have life abundantly! I have often heard or read that most people have a "form of godliness." I know this to be true; they never really come into the full acknowledgement of the things of God. They never have an intimate vertical relationship with You. Why? I think most people are afraid to give up something, or they just want the good things of God and not the sacrifices. They do not want to change what they feel or "their" ways. With God, "change" is inevitable. You cannot truly know God and remain the same.

We were ultimately born into sin. Our nature is to sin. With God, our nature has to change; it cannot stay the same. For example, our first reaction to someone who has hurt us is to hurt them back, or if someone strikes us we want to strike them back because of our nature. We have to put our nature under submission and walk in a new direction, in the direction of God. However, when the going gets tough, the tough get going. What an understatement. With God, when the going get tough, the truly tough get tougher. They hang in there, and they do not faint. They continue on the road that ultimately leads to heaven.

I used to think that I could fix my marriage and that I could make it work. But today, I know that I cannot. Only God can fix broken hearts, hardened hearts, selfish hearts, and cold hearts. Only God can save this world. The only thing we can do is finish the race, go the distance. The only thing I can do is continue through the marriage and not give up or turn around. I have learned to see things the way they truly are. I am not perfect, and he is not perfect. We both need God. Only God can help us to come together as a couple and stand together as a couple and to really become one. I thought we loved each other, but I have heard over and over that love is never enough. When life, circumstances, money, children, and the devil finish stomping on the relationship, all the love seems so irrelevant, so insignificant in comparison. If two people are not grounded, rooted, and focused on God, Lord have mercy. When it comes down to accepting one another and loving each other unconditionally, only God can give us that capacity, and even then it is still a struggle. "Because we war not with flesh and blood."

If you do not know God and have not experienced His unconditional love, it is impossible to grasp the dynamics. This unconditional love cannot be humanly possible unless there is a right relationship with the Father. That is why there are so many broken relationships in our world today. Lord God, please do not let there be another broken dream, another broken heart, another broken family, and another failed union. The issues are seldom who the two people are, but basically just the issues of life—getting along, acceptance, unselfishness, and unconditional love, and not how someone looks, talks, walks, because the makeup is the same. We all have feelings, opinions, ideas, and imperfections. We just need to know how to find a balance, how to find peace, how to find joy and contentment with each other. That will only come with godly wisdom. I would do anything to save this marriage, but unfortunately, my mate does not feel the same. So basically, I cannot do anything. I can only ride it out and see what the end is going to be.

My spouse told me a year or so ago that the marriage was over, but I still search his eyes for a glimmer of hope when I get a chance. So that is why I stay. That is why I dream of my husband and I together once again loving each other in Jesus' name. I know I loved him from the very first day, and I am not stupid. I know and have always been in touch with my feelings. It was not lust, it was not need, and it was not loneliness or vulnerability. It was God, as I see it today some five years later. I will always love him, even if it is from afar. (That made me cry because at times, it *has* been from afar.) I will always pray for him and pray that God will bless him, no matter what. God gives me this hope, and God gives me hope for tomorrow. If it was not for this hope that God has given me, I would walk right out the door and never look back like many have done. I am not afraid of being alone or taking care of me I have always done that, even as a child. I know how to lick my wounds, I learned early!

Love, Your daughter, Rkh

June 10, 1999

Dear God, what have I done to deserve such a mess? There is trouble on both sides. The Bible says trials and tribulations come to make you strong. I guess I will be Hercules soon. I know my husband and I need to pray together, but how do you get someone to pray with you? He has not responded to that at all. I asked him if we could start praying together. He never answered. I knew what the Bible said, but I just wanted that man! I was blinded; I really thought he loved me. I did think that. I thought we would be together and go to church and just grow to love Jesus more and more. I also thought we would raise the children together, but that did not happen either. Sometimes I wish I could just say, "Okay God, I made a mistake," and then God would just erase it away. But it does not work that way, and if it did, would we try everything and never learn from our mistakes? I have cried so many tears. I have cried and cried some more, and when I feel like I can't cry again, I cry again. Then I say, "I am not going to cry anymore over him," but I end up crying over him. I have cried so many times. I have cried so hard. I know that there is a lesson in this. God is preparing me. He is making me tough. I want to be able to stand regardless and not cry, to be strong, not to hurt, not to want him, not to desire him, and to dish out to him what he is giving me. That would give new meaning to reciprocity! But I cannot. When I try, I feel awful because I know what the Bible says. God taught me how to love, agape-style. Why I chose to give it to a man that does not understand that kind of love and cannot give it back, I do not understand. Woe is me! They mistreated Jesus, and He was the Son of God and was spotless. I know that I am not spotless. I know I will be mistreated. Thank You, God, for being here for me. Love, Your daughter, Rkh

June 19, 1999

Dear God, five years have gone by. How can you bring back those feelings? Why do I relive those days of when I fell in love with him? I think of those times, and they blind me to reality. I cannot understand, and I guess I never will understand how you just stop loving someone. How do you just give up on a marriage? I never gave up on the first one until that very day he left. I wanted him to leave. I asked him to leave. I begged him to leave. That is what I wanted, but I would probably have never left if it had been up to me. I am not sure what that is all about. But hopefully one day, I will better understand myself and God's plan for my life. I am basically doing the same thing with this marriage: hoping that one day he will fall back in love with me or that he will just walk out. I do not understand why he just does not walk out. It is hard living here together.

I have fallen in love with him over and over again. I do not understand it myself. Reality is, he is trying to drive me away. Everything is just my fault. The debt, the bills, the relationship—all are my fault. That is just not true. God, please give me strength to leave this alone and let You handle this situation. Help me to accept the way things are until You fix it. God, help me to not seem so desperate and to step away and give us both time to think before we make any decisions. Please, Lord, give me the strength, because I know only You can fix this situation or change it. Help me not to go running back and begging and apologizing or desiring to sleep with him. I have done all of the above too many times. He already knows all he has to do is just try—just come back to this room and touch me, and he knows that he can have me. But at this time he apparently does not want that.

I guess right now I am feeling like a loser with a second marriage gone sour. But I know I am not the only person who has gone through this. I never wanted it to go sour. I asked my husband (or I told him) we needed to start praying together. He never answered. Prayer changes things. I am praying for strength right now to be strong and endure this heartache, this hardship, and this brokenness in my marriage. I am afraid of what might happen. The Bible says, "Do not fear." I think the worst part is failing. I think I have almost forgotten how it feels to be loved, held, wanted, or needed. Flash back—Delta ball... I remember we were dancing, I was very tense or had my guard up due to all the issues between us. I did not want to let my guard down. We were slow dancing, but we were not touching each other. There was so much tension between us. He said to me, "I am not going to bite you." He said it so softly, so kindly, so gently. I thought I was hearing things. My heart melted, and I relaxed and fell in love with him all over again. I think that was in February or March, about three months ago. I keep thinking of that night. I have no doubt about my love, even tonight. I loved him the first time I saw him. When I got to know him, I loved him even more. He is a very special person, and any woman would love him. The question is, what woman would he love? I know he loved his ex-girl-friend. He told me that he loved her and that he wanted to marry her. I wish he could love me that way. Sometimes I think he still loves her, and he just married me to try to get back at her.

Tonight he is in his room alone. I am in this room alone, and that is the way he has wanted it for the last month or so. We should work out all our differences no matter what. I am willing. Love, Rkh

August 14, 1999

Dear God, I cannot believe I have not written since June 19. I am in Northfolk, Virginia, sitting by an indoor pool sipping a piña colada. It is very relaxing, and it has been nice, though not my atmosphere. The two-hour boatride was a disco. Like I said, not my atmosphere. I am here with Sandy and her secret boyfriend. I really do not mind, for I can entertain myself. She deserves the best, but more than that, I wish she knew You better. I wish *I* knew You better. It is what I long for, an even closer walk with You.

Every day, You show me more and more how dependent I am on You—how vulnerable I am to this world. I thank You for Your protection because I know it is only You. As far as my life, I am trying to concentrate on You, to focus on You, and be closer and more spiritual. I know that is the only way I am going to be able to stay focused and make it until Jesus comes. In a way, my marriage is so much of my fault. I can be so stubborn and even heartless at times. God, we really need You in our marriage. If we do not get right with You, then I know our marriage is doomed. You know, God, it is like my first marriage. I knew that if we both did not get right with You, the marriage would dissolve, and it did. I am asking, "Is there someone who loves me enough to just do what is necessary to salvage the marriage? Am I supposed to be married twice? Was I supposed to have re-married?" I really believed that it was the right thing to do. I could not have loved a man more than I loved him. Maybe I put him first. To be honest, I did. I know You are a jealous God. Now, I want God to be first because I have learned through all these difficult times that You are number one and that You change not. You are the same today, yesterday, and forever. My husband changes from day to day.

On the 17th of August, it will be our sixth anniversary. I will be here, and he will be there. I want to call him. I really do. God, lead me. Holy Spirit, guide me, because I truly do not know what to do. I just want to tell him I miss him. I do not ever know if I am welcomed back or if the alarm and the locks will be changed. But, God is good, and I know that all things happen for a reason. I miss my children, and I am ready to go back to my life. God, guide me and let Your will be done in my life, not *my* will, but only yours. Love, Your daughter, Rkh

Afterthought: Bless us as we return to our own homes. Go before us as You always have, and, Lord, clear the paths of any obstacles that may try to prevent us from returning safely. Bless my children, all my family, and my friends. Rkh

August 30, 1999

Dear God, here it is five a.m. on a Monday morning. I cannot sleep, or I slept too long during the day. I did get at least two-and-a-half hours of napping after church. It felt good. Lord, where do I begin? Nothing's changed at home. There are still the marriage, children, and home issues going on. He is still as cold to me as before I left. I would not doubt it if he just plain wishes I would go away and never come back. I wish he would tell me what he wants. I wish he would tell me to go, to leave and never to come back, but he does not. He will not. Why do I need him to tell me that when he has said it in so many ways? I cannot believe I could be so stupid. So much of me says, "Run, Forrest, run."

I hope that things will change. I hope that I am not fooling myself. "It would be not trusting God if I left," I rationalize. There are so many questions to be answered, like why? how? where? when? God, I have to have faith in You; that must be the ultimate decision. I must believe that "all things work together for good for those that love the Lord and are the called according to his purpose." I cannot give up; I have seen God work things out too many times in my life. I know I have. Why do I think He will forsake me now? The devil is a liar. Why would God bring me this far only to leave me? He has told me His plan, and it is a plan of blessings. He has given me hope for tomorrow. He has told me I am blessed, and my house is blessed. He has spoken this to me. I know He has. This doubt and fear is not from God. "Get thee behind me, Satan. God has not given us a spirit of fear, but a spirit of love and peace and a sound mind." He did not say it would be easy, but I know He has spoken His word. Lord, give me the strength to endure, give me the power and might to hold on. I believe in miracles. Love, Your daughter, Rkh

Afterthought: I know God asked me if I believed in miracles over and over again while I was home one morning in North Carolina. I said, "Yes, yes, yes, I believe in miracles."

September 1, 1999

I know God told me I was blessed, and my house is blessed. God has worked out many blessings in my life, in every area, in every way.

God, bless my son in the Great Lakes. Please have him contact his mother soon. I plead the blood of Jesus over him, that he is safe and doing well. Thank You, Lord.

I ask, God, that You bless my husband and send to him words of wisdom, words of encouragement, and words of salvation so that he may come to know you as his personal Savior. I ask that you show him how to love, to care, to forgive, and to be humble, considerate, and kind.

I ask, Lord, that You bless all the children's going in and coming out, their schoolwork and their attitude about schoolwork, their minds, and most of all, Lord, protect their love for You. Let it be pure, genuine love for You. Bless my daughter. Please put Your protection around her. Help her to see You more clearly. Bless her on her job, in her home, and everywhere she goes. Help her find a true Christian mate that can help her raise her son. Thank You, Jesus.

Bless my grandson; help him to grow emotionally secure, strong, and healthy. Protect him as he goes to daycare. Bless all he does. Thank You, Lord. Bless all the children; protect their minds and bodies wherever they go. I ask that Your angels encamp around them and protect them from evil. Thank You, Jesus!

Bless all my coworkers and my neighborhood, Lord! Bless all the people and families, that they my see You as the one and only true God. Bless marriages, children, relationships, jobs, and wellbeing. Thank You, Jesus! Love, Rkh

September 3, 1999

Seven more days, and I go. That is unbelievable. What sense does that make? Just run. Is that what I will do? There are so many things to consider, so many reasons to run, and so many reasons to stay. The reason to stay is selfish, I know. It is so hard to understand, so hard to comprehend, so hard to conceive that there will be no "me and you." No matter what that meant, it is all I have known for the last six years, and now in seven days, I will pack up and go and live alone. That makes me so awfully sad. It is a like a dull ache, like something you hope will go away because sooner or later it will become a great pain. It is like a pain that you will have to seek treatment for if left unattended. Can I handle this? I know the first weeks it will be very hard not coming home, even though I do not feel at

home; and as time goes by, it does not get any better. I certainly have not seen him much or talked with him much lately. He makes it very clear whose house this is. "Anyone else, please step aside." There are so many reasons to go. I am so afraid I will not be brave enough that day.

I know this needs to happen. God, I know something has to, or it will get worse as time goes on. I never would have believed this would happen; yet it is happening right before my eyes. He has done everything in his power to push me away, to let me know he does not want to try to salvage our marriage. God, it is in Your hands. But God, I really feel I cannot stay. I am afraid that something might happen—something like what happened two days ago. That was ugly. I was ugly, and I really felt like busting down all the doors with that hammer. (Lord, You know what happened, and You stepped in before anyone got hurt. Thank You so much for keeping me in my right mind.) It was my fault. I let him get the best of me, but You interceded and worked everything out. I admit we probably went over our heads with this house, but we can afford it. We just have to work together, but that is way out of the picture. We have to accept each other's ways and learn to love each other unconditionally. We have to treat each other well because this is home, and home should be a place where everybody should feel comfortable and live peacefully. I never want to argue like that again. I feel like I have no other choice, like my back is up against the wall. I wish it did not have to happen, but it is happening.

I have put money on an apartment and have a move-in date, I have already made arrangements, and on September 10, it will happen. God, will You intervene this time because I really do not want to go? There are things that I should not have done. I just tried to do what was right, even though it turned out so wrong. Now I have regrets. Now I have to deal with it because in seven days I will be gone. I am tired of locked doors, separate families, separate bills, separate dinners, separation, bad tempers, bad attitudes, bad feelings, bad arguments, not speaking, saying "I love you" and getting no response. How long am I supposed to take this? How long can it go on like this? How long before something happens, before my son loses hope, feels bad about himself, has low self-esteem, loses sight, believes what he sees, is affected by the words, gets angry, fights back, stops loving, blames me, or blames himself? I go. I must go. Love, Rkh

Afterthought: I do not want to get a divorce. I want to work out our differences. I want to be his wife because I made that oath, that commitment not only to him, but also to God. I will not break that commitment. Hopefully, we can work out our differences after I move. It will give us the much-needed time apart. I am still his wife and will be there to work it out if he wants to try. So far, he has given me no indication of reconciliation, even though he knows I could be moving out.

September 25, 1999

Dear Lord, It has been a while, and you know everything. I am still praying and believing you for miracles in relationships, children, health, and the issues of life. I know You are God. I know You know all things, and all things are possible through You. You keep showing me that table You are preparing in front of my enemies. I know that I might just be hindering this, but Lord, I know You will bless me in spite of myself. Change me, Lord, and help me to stop thinking that others need to change. I need to change too. Ultimately, it is all about me and you dealing with me right where I am. Help me to be closer to You and to put You first. Then things will change. Rkh

September 26, 1999

Where do I begin? In the womb? I wonder why my life is the way it is. What have I done so wrong? If I knew, I would change things. I would do things differently. But I really do not know. Am I terribly insecure? I know the Lord Jesus, and I have the Father-daughter relationship between God and me. I wonder why it seems like some people have husbands that go with them to church, that love the Lord, and they work out all their difficulties. Since I have known the Lord, I have always wanted a good strong Christian man—a man who loves God and believes that His Son died for him, and a man who actually appreciates Jesus' death and crucifixion. It was not an easy sacrifice. My lust and selfishness blinded me. He was so good-looking and seemed so sincere. He seemed so dedicated in attending church every Sunday. I loved him from the beginning. Even though we had our times when we were dating, I loved everything about him—even the things that were not perfect. Besides that, he seemed to love me like that too. We had some great times when it was right. I was smitten. We were together all the time. It was like we could not get enough of each other, and we clung to each other even in the hard times. It was never really over even though we were angry. Even now when we are angry at each other, we know it will never really be over. We were so caught up with each other at that time. I trusted and believed in him. When he quit his job, I did not flinch because I knew what kind of man he was and that he was too responsible not to find another one. He found a better job than the one he quit. He drove me to work and picked me up every day until he found another job. I lived for the moments we were together. Now, six years later, we do not even have a relationship. What happened?

Maybe he is just turned off by the hard times and is waiting for me to get tired and leave. He no longer loves me or desires me. That is a hard pill to swallow; to think the man you love does not love you will make even the strongest woman really insecure. I still love him, and I know that I will always love him. I saw something so cold in his eyes when we met at Taco Bell during lunch. It really got my attention, and I keep wondering what I saw or if I even really did see what I thought I saw. He no longer goes to church anywhere. I figure he has given up on God, on me, and on our marriage. Maybe that is what I saw—defeat. I have never seen defeat in anyone's eyes before. I hope I am wrong. That makes me feel really sorry for everything. I never ever wanted to hurt him. But obviously I did, time and time again. I wish we could talk, but we do not any longer. We still go out. We still meet for lunch, dinner, go to movies, etc. But the love we had has gone away. I hope we can find it again someday. I guess we are waiting for the other to call it quits.

I sometimes think that I should have left on September 10. Everything was set, but I was afraid, torn, and unsure of what to do, so I stayed. Things have not changed, and he never knew how close I was to leaving. I am praying for a change. I am praying that I be Christlike in this matter, that I can back off and give him time and let God do his job. I keep trying, nagging, acting stupid, craving attention (positive or negative), hurting, and crying; like one day I can deal with it and then the next I cannot. God, please intervene in this marriage. Show us the way. Change me, change him, and change our situation tonight! Oh, Lord God, please hear my prayer. I know You will never forsake me. Give me strength to do the right things and say the right things in my life. So many times I do not. I love You, God, and I know You hear my cry. I know You have heard my cry every time, and I know You care about what I am going through. Please, Lord God, help us have a closer walk with you as a family. Love, Your daughter, Rkh

December 31, 1999

New Years Eve—I am alone. I came from the prayer tower and taking communion at Highland. My spouse is somewhere (not here), and from what he said, I guess he is doing what he wants to do. I will not repeat his exact words, but they were harsh, very harsh. But, I have to be strong. God, grant me the serenity to accept the things I cannot change, the courage to change the things I can, and the wisdom to know the difference (a prayer from my childhood). Into the new millennium 2000—serve God, trust God, be obedient. That is what I need. Bless my family in Jesus' name, Amen. Love, Rkh

January 1, 2000

The New Year came in just like any other year. I thought about all the hype, about Christmas and New Year's. But I did hope Jesus would come. I mean, that *was* the media frenzy—that so much would go wrong...Y2K...blah, blah, blah. But Jesus did not come, so it is not time. Life goes on. Some are not ready. Honestly, I am not ready; I have so many flaws in my life, in my personality. I have a long road ahead of me with so many errors in my ways. Please, Lord, change me so I can be like Your Son Jesus Christ. This will not be a year of complaints. This will be a growth period in my spirituality. It has been on the back burner long enough. This year, it will be first. My New Year's resolutions are: be a tither, exercise, drink plenty of water, keep my faith, not run behind anyone for love but to love myself and my Lord no matter what, to be a kinder gentler person, to not be so ill-tempered and not complain so much, to love Jesus with all my heart and soul, to attend church at least two times a week if not three, to love my enemies and do unto others, and to pray for those who spitefully use me. Rkh

September 25, 2000
Dear God, nine months later, I am separated from my husband. We are living apart. I have nothing to say.

October 1, 2000
Dear God! Here I am sitting at my desk in my new apartment. I guess I will spend a lot of time here. Besides, I will be taking my last classes prior to graduating. It has been a long, tedious road, but I am thankful to You for giving me the strength to make it this far. A lot has happened. It seems silly writing to You because You know already and You knew already. You know everything; you are the Alpha and the Omega. You know all about me, and You know my destination. Where will I go? I am praying to Wilmington, North Carolina as an accountant.

Well, my husband and I are officially separated now. I moved out over the weekend. He was in Miami. I sold most of my furniture because it was too heavy to move. I am purchasing new not-so-heavy furniture soon. I do not feel bad about it. (Thank You, God.) I am disappointed and hate that we took each other through so much before I finally moved out. I realize now that at this time, it cannot work. I realize that we probably should have waited to get married. We both had too many other issues. We were only thinking about ourselves and our love for each other. The timing was not right. We should have just dated. I do not know why we were in such a hurry to get married. Well, honestly I *do* know why. I was so bound up in guilt about having a sexual relationship and not being married. I was under really strong condemnation, for although I tried to refrain from having sex, (as we both did), the majority of the time it was me that gave in and practically attacked him. I knew we loved each other so. We were both single, we loved each other, and so we got married. We did not even think about the issues of having an extended family, finances, and the ups and downs of living together that all couples go through. Even though we are living apart, I hope this is not the end of our relationship. I would love to still date him. Can you date someone you are married to? Is it called "dating"? I hope that one day You will bring us back together again, but not like it was before—not with all the strife, anger, bitterness, pressure, tension, and difficulties. I know that You can change a human being. Lord, get rid of the selfishness, anger, and pain that were in our marriage. Bring us back to-gether, Lord, so that we may glorify Your name, and love and worship You all the days of our lives. Let Your will be done. It is in Your hands. Send a calming spirit to my husband so that he may come to know You, Lord, and have a personal relationship with You. Send people, messages, and songs so that he may be saved and run to You saying, "I yield, I yield." I do not mind being single at all. That is certainly not my issue. It is just I do not desire to be single, nor do I desire to be separated from my husband. I am enjoying myself and the peace and quiet. Our home was filled with so much tension. Well, I am enjoying my son again and enjoying not being in those uncom-fortable, awkward moments. I do not miss the arguing or the mess. Sometimes I wonder why I took it so long. I guess I wanted it to work be-cause I believed we truly loved each other, but only You know whom he loves and if he ever really truly loved me. I cannot worry about that at this point. God, thank You for Your grace and mercy and protect me, Lord God, and "surely goodness and mercy will follow me all the days of my life." I love You with all my heart. Your child, Rkh (You know me!) Love, Your lost sheep.

No Date

Dear God, thank You for Jean. She has helped me through several of my classes. With all that has happened, if it was not for her, I do not know how I would have made it through these hard accounting courses. She has been a godsend. Please let me bless her with a nice dinner soon. I am here my third day in my apartment. I must say it is nice, although he is always in the back of my mind. I cannot believe I did this. As I read back through this journal, I know that my actions are justified because of the things I went through with him. But, I can't help how I feel, and I miss him. I al-ways will, but life must go on. I hope this makes me a more humble person. I know I have my own issues. Surprisingly, I do not even feel alone. I pray that You, my Lord, will put this marriage back together one day. Until then, I will wait. We both need time to think and to look back on the things that have happened. Lord, You know what is best for me. You know if he will ever be the husband that he should be, a godly husband and man. I know You can change the hardest heart. Bless him, Lord, in all he does.

How long can he run? Where can he hide? He has lost his wife. He has not called. What is there to say right now? Lord, I love you, and I know that You are always with me. Help me through this and help me to be all that you would have me to be. Goodnight. Love, Your daughter, Rkh

October 3, 2000

Dear God, this is the start of my second journal. It has been a couple of years since I started. There have been long gaps during this time. I am alone, but not lonely. It seems so strange being alone—an eerie kind of quiet that seems like at any given moment will be interrupted. I guess I have to get used to it. My son is happy; I am glad of that. He is a king, and he deserves to feel at home, loved, and wanted. I am sure he feels this way now. I know his grades will improve. As far as my husband is concerned, I do wonder how he feels and what he is thinking. I know that is not my concern right now. I have other things to be concerned about—work, school, and taking care of my son and me. I like it, sad to say. I could not ever see myself without my husband, and I hated the thought of that and of leaving the house. I do not feel like I did during the first divorce. Then, I hated the thought of being single. Now I know that being alone is better when you cannot find peace in a relationship. I will take my time and get to know me and my God. I feel like this is too peaceful, and I should feel rotten. But I do not, and if God does not change my husband and bring him out of his ways, I know that it is over between us. Miracles do come true. I only wish blessings to him, even though we had a rough time. He actually got it all really, and that is okay, as odd as it seems. He got the house, the car, and even the dog, and even though that may not seem fair, for some strange reason it is not all that important to me. Because I know God will "supply all my needs according to his riches and glory." I trust You, God, with all my heart and my soul. I know You will give me a double portion of anything I have lost—even a double saved, doubled filled, Holy Ghost brother when the time comes and if it is in your plan for my life. Goodnight, Holy Spirit, Jesus, and Father God. Love, Your daughter, Rkh

October 4, 2000

Dear God, I went to church tonight for the first time since I moved. I really enjoyed it, and I am looking forward to going back Sunday. Father, I am so glad you are with me. You give me peace and joy. Things should be awful, but You are in the midst, showing me how You will sustain Your people if they trust and believe in You. I am separated from the man I love, my husband, and I have not heard from him since I left. As awful as that sounds, I know that Your Word says, "All things work together for good for those that love the Lord and are called according to his purpose." Glory to God! I know He has great things for me. I love You, Father. Your daughter, Rkh

October 5, 2000

My son's fifteenth birthday is coming on October 7. I am going to take him out to dinner and get him something very special. I love him, and I am sorry I have taken him through so much. I do not know what I was thinking. Well, I got my hair done today. Thank God. I was so glad and thankful. I do not have to worry about that for a while. I thought of my husband a lot today. I mean, I thought of us together, and I remembered how nice it was being with him. I want to say but...but what? I know that everything that happens now is in God's will; it is in God's hands. I even thought of calling him, but I know I might be intruding in God's affairs. Lord, You know I am good about that. I must be patient and wait on the Lord. He has to fix this. Although I love him and miss him, I know we have many issues to deal with right now. He needs time to decide, to think, to hear God, and make a move toward godliness. Without God, I know this marriage will not work. The children, the dog, the locked doors, the division, the anger, the manipulation, the control, and the selfishness, I cannot take any longer. I certainly do not want to take my son back to the same environment ever again.

I do wonder if he misses me, though. Is this what he really wanted? Is he full of regret? How is he handling it? Is he hurt, angry, devastated, or is he relieved? I wonder. We were the couple who had it all but couldn't get it right. It is hard. It was hard, and I know we both suffered. God, please bless my son. I plead the blood of Jesus over him for protection, that positivism, and godliness will always surround him. I am tired right now, and it has been a long day. Goodnight, God. I love You, and thank You for Your grace and Your mercy. I know that I am really being wishywashy right about now. I want him, I don't… I miss him, I don't… I must seem like an emotional wreck. Love, Your daughter (I will say my prayers). Rkh

October 6, 2000

Dear God, I had a nice day. I picked my grandson up at school. We got off at 3:31, which is always a joy for some reason—just fifty-nine minutes earlier than normal, but it is a good feeling. It makes me feel like I can work a little while longer. I took the kids for Chinese in honor of my son's birthday. I am going to buy him something he really wants. I bought a computer, but I need someone to help me put it and the stand together. I have to wait for someone to make time. I hate having to bug someone, though. That is one thing I hate about being single. However, on the other hand, maybe it would be days before a husband would get around to it either.

I talked to my mother, but I did not tell her about the separation. I did not want to hear the disappointment in her voice. I do not know what the future holds, but I am just bracing myself. I love God, and I know He orders my steps, that He protects and guides me. He gives me peace in the midst of the storm. It is good to be at peace; at a place you can call your own, whether it is a house or an apartment, where you know you can find comfort and where your child can find comfort and peace as well. I had a strange thought about going to court and getting the house and an awful thought that I repented for. The devil is a liar! I love the Lord, and I would rather have Jesus than anything in this world.

I thought of him today, but I did not long for him as yesterday. For some reason, I keep thinking that we will run into each other soon. I did not move far away because I did not want my son to have to change schools. I know when the time is right, we will talk. When all thoughts are clear and all the tension and pain have subsided within ourselves, maybe we can see clearly again. I am praying that we can maintain a relationship and save our marriage. He has not contacted me yet, so I continue to wonder what he is thinking and feeling. Two people have to care about each other and work at making a marriage work—one person cannot keep a marriage together. Goodnight. I am tired and I want to rest and become refreshed (one of God's greatest gifts). We do not have to live in yesterday's grace and mercies because He gives us new mercies every morning with renewed strength. So, we can endure whatever we have to each day. Love, Rkh

October 7, 2000

Today was my son's birthday. I hope that he had fun and realized he is very special. The days are going okay; of course, I am always kind of pinching myself to see if I am dreaming. Going on without my spouse is not easy. I guess that is neither here nor there at this time. It seems strange just going on with your life when a vital part of your life is suddenly gone. I will say suddenly because, although I have talked about the increasing division between us over the years, I never actually thought it would happen, especially since I prayed to God to fix my marriage. I really do not understand what has happened, but I must go on. Even though I feel like questioning God, I will not. I know that He is much wiser that I am. On the opposite end of the spectrum, there are things that one could say are advantages to being alone. One is that there are no issues to handle but your own. Another is that there is no drama. I do not miss being in that house that the devil tried to make a hell for me, and I certainly do not miss the drama. I am looking forward to going to church tomorrow so that I may give thanks and honor to God. I know that He will provide everything I need according to His riches and glory. I know I am blessed going in and coming out. I will rest now, for it has been a long day. Thank You, Lord, for Your strength. I look forward for the grace and new mercies for tomorrow. I am sure I will need it. Love, Your daughter, Rkh

October 10, 2000

Today was a holiday. It was nice being off, and I enjoyed just doing much of nothing. I thought of him a lot again today. I am finally realizing that we are actually separated, and there is no earthly reason why we should even get back together. It is the way it is now, and I cannot change it. I told my son I was sad today, and he said that well, maybe he is sad too. I wonder if he is. I wonder if he is afraid like I am, or is he glad to have us out of his hair. I guess there is no time to cry over spilt milk, even though to call it "spilt milk" is a vast understatement. I know that things will always happen for the best to those who love the Lord. I love You, Lord, and I give my life, my hopes, and my dreams to You. Please guide me and help me to know that even when it hurts and I am brokenhearted, You, oh God, will not put more on me than I can bear. Love, Your daughter, Rkh

October 12, 2000
  Dear Father, I did not write last night. I was very upset and tired last night. I know why now. I had a visitor last night, and that is the reason why I could not shake the lonely feeling I felt. I always feel that way right before I have my cycle. I thought I was upset more than usual because he called and the conversation did not go the way I wanted it to. I almost wanted him to beg me to come back and say how hurt he was and that he missed me. But he did not even ask how I was or if I was okay after about two weeks, an unexpected move, and a separation—after all that happened. I was hurt, and his call appeared to be about him and his car insurance and things like that. I have to get insurance for the car, and I will still have to pay his medical because I just cannot cancel the policy, not that I would anyway. That was the extent of our conversation. I did not talk because I did not feel good anyway. I was tired of his selfishness. Oh, he will help me pay the medical—yeah, right. Oh top of that and my cycle, it was a rough day—one of the roughest. God is able, though, and it is only in His strength that I move and breathe. I called him back to ask how long I had to get insurance, and he said "Through this month." I also asked about my CDs. I wanted to get them. He said, "I do not see a problem with that."
  Just what I needed—a civil separation! I guess he thinks he has got the best out of the marriage and actually he did (the house, the car, and the dog). But he does not have You, Lord, and for that reason, he does not have the best. "What does it profit a man to gain the whole world and lose his soul?" Besides, I would rather have You, Lord. Know matter what anyone thinks I know I am the winner and I have the ultimate victory. I will have a better day tomorrow, and each day will be even better because I know a MAN...a great MAN!...a true and living God...the lover of my soul! Love, Your daughter, Rkh

No Date

Dear God, I saw him today. I did not realize how much I really missed seeing him, and we were together. It felt so different, like boyfriend and girlfriend, but we know we are husband and wife. There was not much tension as there normally is, and we made love like before in the earlier years. I know that he missed me, too, and he said he loves me. I do not know what is going to happen, but I know that at this time we have to be apart. I miss him, but I know I have to raise my son, and I know the issues we had when we lived in the same house. He said that we were going to work something out. He said we had to. I am content to be this way for a while until the air clears. I kissed him passionately when I left; I wonder why we had not kissed like that in months. We have always had great, passionate lovemaking but have felt awkward toward each other outside the bedroom. It reminded me of when we first met. I hope we can start over and iron out all of our differences. I would still leave for a while if I get the job in Wilmington, North Carolina. I know it would be hard, but I think at this time we could sustain a long-distance relationship, Lord willing. Thank You, Lord, for tonight. I mean, after all, we are married, and it is okay. We both needed to be together. I did not want to talk either, and I know that will come later. We do have so many issues. Love, Your daughter, Rkh

No Date

Dear God, today started out rough, really rough. I thought of him a lot, and that made me very sad earlier. It made me depressed. My son made me angry because he is not keeping his room clean, and I do not think he is doing his homework either. I still have to make him study, clean up, etc. I hit him and yelled at him really badly. I cried about it later. I know that it had to do with everything that is happening and all the other stress of being alone and trying to raise a teenager alone. Living without my husband is so strange. When I went over to the house, he had taken my picture down from over the fireplace and only had his picture there. I did not say anything about it, but it hurt. After all, it is still *our* house. I do not know why I am here when I know I want to be with him. I cannot change things. They are the way they are, and I do not know what to do about it. I am just trying to live each day as best I can and lean on the Father, the Son, and the Holy Ghost. Church tomorrow, thank God!

Maybe I will at least talk to him tomorrow to see how he is. His brother is very ill, and he had another busy day today. I did not speak with him at all. I hope I will tomorrow. If not, I will call him on Monday. I pray that he is okay. I am just so sorry he gave up on us and our marriage, and also on God. I hope he finds his way soon. He has to change, and as much as I would love to go home some day, I know that there has to be a significant change in our marriage and the way we interact with each other and interact with our families. The love of God has to be in the midst of every decision we make for the rest of our lives. No matter how brokenhearted I am, I know that we need Jesus, we need a church home, and we need to pray together and worship together and be on one accord. When I look back, things were getting out of control. They were ridiculous. Things were happening uncontrollably, and I was very afraid.

I am afraid now that our marriage will never be right and that we will never live together again. I know if it is the Lord's will, I do not have to see it or know how it will get fixed—all I have to do is believe. I miss him so much, and I truly fell in love with him when I met him. That is no lie. I love him so much and that is why it took so long for me to leave. He told me a long time ago that our marriage was over, and I just did not want to hear nor believe it. I do not understand that at all. That is the mystery in divorce for me. I mean, you live together, you are each other's everything, and then one day it is all over and you go your separate ways. It is almost devastating, especially when we were so close at one time that we held hands so tightly, we held on to each other for dear life, and at one time it felt like it was us against the world. Where do broken hearts go? Lord, let Your will be done on earth as it is in heaven. Please, Lord, give me the strength to do all that You say and help me to be obedient to Your Word and glorify Your precious name. I love You, God. You never change; You are always the same. Love, Rkh

No Date

Dear God, today was another struggle. Church was beautiful, as usual, and I know that You are always with me. I need Your help and guidance in every way. My grandchild's father did not pick him up today. I guess I am not surprised at all. I guess I will keep him myself until his mother comes back. She is overseas right now. I will not comment on that issue at this time. There are some very ugly words trying to creep in my spirit right now. I talked with my husband today. We really talked some, and we stopped before it became an argument and a blame game. We did not want to argue or even reflect back on the past. He said he wanted to work on our happiness, to try resolving our issues. I cried, but I am used to crying these days. I miss him so much. We need to resolve a lot of children issues as well. Can they be resolved? I will not go back until my son is finished with high school. That is four years from now. I will wait. I love him, and I love my son. Even if I leave and take a job somewhere else, I will come back in four years. I love him so much, and the sound of his voice makes me shiver. I cannot imagine someone else knowing him that well, knowing him inti-mately. He is my husband, and we are having some serious problems right now, but I know God will fix them. I know He will because He is the lover of my soul. I really do not like living without him. I loved to cuddle up be-side him at night against his back and feel his body against mine. I miss holding his hand while we made love. I miss that. I hope we can spend some time together soon and go out or something. I guess I will sleep now. I love You, Jesus, and I love You, Holy Spirit. I will go and pray now. I love my grandchild, and I love all my children. Love, Your daughter, Rkh

No Date

Dear God, I just left my husband, and it was nice being with him. I do not know what I am doing. I guess he will never know how he broke my heart. I feel right now that he used me and is continuing to use me. He has everything—the house, the car, the dog—and I just come and go, come and go. I do not even feel like it is my house anymore or that he is even my husband any longer. I just want to leave, God, just leave it all and get over him.

We bought all those things together, and we were supposed to share them together. He does not even know how I feel, and I will not tell him because these are my feelings, and I do not want him to know me that deeply anymore. He promised to be with me through thick or thin, and he was not. When things got bad, he basically made it so bad for me that I had to leave. Now, he wants me to be with him and then go home and leave him to his peaceful house afterward. Now, he wants me to be at his beck and call. I guess he is afraid that I will find someone else or something, but he does not care enough to try again. I cannot do that anyway, but it hurts to not be able to move back home, and it hurts even more that he is okay with it. At least we should talk about it. We do not talk about it at all. When I leave, I want him to hurt, to long for me, and to want me to stay. I want to break his heart and let him know how it feels for someone you love to just squash all your hopes and dreams. I know that is mean, God, and please forgive me, but that is how I feel right about now. I am really upset. I hope I will not feel like this next time I write. I do love him with all my heart, and I just wish he would have loved me enough to try to make our marriage work regardless of the issues we had.

When I get a job offer, I am going to take it. There is really nothing for me here. What am I supposed to do? Stay here four or five years and act like we are not married, live separately, and go visit him, make love, and tell each other we love each other as long as it is not inconvenient? I cannot do that. I want to move back home. If moving back home is impossible, then at least I can work on my career. God, I am so sorry we are apart, but I know it is best for everyone involved. So why am I complaining, right? Rkh

No Date

Dear God, I want to see him, but I have my grandson, and my son has gone to the church for some activities. Then he will spend the night with my girlfriend's son and will not be back until tomorrow. So I will not be able to see him tonight. I guess I will see him tomorrow night. I did my homework (some of it), and I am glad I did. I need to concentrate on school. I am excited about graduating on May 17, so I want to make really good grades from now on. My overall GPA is 3.29. I wanted it to be at least a 3.4 or better. I love You, God, Jesus, and the Holy Spirit. It is not always about him or school or work. It is about me being aware that You are so real in my life. I do not understand how some people cannot see it, feel it, and long for a relationship with You. That, I do not understand at all.

My husband and I attended a play last week. It was an awesome play with an awesome message of salvation. After the play, I thought everyone in that building should be changed, mind, body, and soul. I prayed that it did change some lives.

Believe it or not, I had an interview with someone from the Pentagon in Washington, D.C. Now I am thoroughly impressed. Where will I go? It is so terribly exciting to have these opportunities, this challenge, and be so close to my degree. Besides, my career here is going nowhere fast. I cannot see staying here and not progressing. I am one semester shy of getting my degree, and I have sacrificed so much for this degree and I also owe student loans that I have to pay back. I have to have the means to pay the loans back and take care of my family. I am excited as far as that. My husband had a chance to be a husband to me and to be a stepfather to my children. It seemed as if everything I loved, he totally tried to take advantage of and destroy. I was not perfect, but I did try, and I loved him enough to accept things as they were until I realized that things would not get better. They were only getting worse. That was very heartbreaking, but God, You were there, and You are still here. You change not. You love me unconditionally, and that is the only thing that matters right now.

When I get that job offer, I am going, and I know truly that "mercy and grace will follow me all the days of my life." I love You, God, and I put all my hope and trust in You and not man or material things. I love my husband, and I hope one day we will be reconciled together and be a family. It is in Your hands, God. Only You know, and only You can make things right. It goes back to being unequally yoked. Fix my marriage, Lord, and bring us back together as one in Christ's name. Amen! Love, Your daughter, Rkh

December 31, 2000

New Year's Rocking Eve 2000… Sometimes I go back and read the things I wrote, and I just shake my head. Sometimes I seem so unstable, so unsure, but the one thing is that you have always come through for me. I thank You, Lord, for that. I thank You, Lord, for keeping me safe from harm and for keeping me sane. Through it all, I know that I have grown, and when I read back, it just encourages me more to keep going on. I am actually keeping an account of my spiritual growth. How awesome is that? This shows how unstable we really are as humans and why we need God so much. Reading the things I wrote previously seems odd. I tell you, it seems over the last several years I have been an emotional wreck. Yet I have continued to function, work, go to school, etc. I need to know that it is all because of God and God only. I feel like a basketcase when I read over some of the things, and now I am wondering why on New Year's Rocking Eve, I am still sad over the state of my marriage. It seems like if I go back and read all the things I have written I should have been over this a long time ago. Yet I sit here not terribly depressed, hurt, and not really angry at all with anyone. At times, I even feel foolish to have endured so much. But I told my son the other day that "I would have rather have loved and to have lost than to never have loved at all," as corny as it sounds.

Sometimes I wonder why people cannot grasp love at all. It seems so simple to me. You love someone, so you treat him or her with kindness, respect, and no matter what they do, you love them. You work and talk about your problems and come to a conclusion, and you abide by that. What is so hard? But the way the world operates, it is hard to grasp such an absurd thing. It is nonsense to the world. Maybe it was nonsense to me before I became a Christian and found that relationship with Jesus. I loved both husbands and do not know what happened. But I am not angry about it either.

My sorrow comes mainly from the thought of going through a second marriage that appears to be a failure. I want to kick myself and say, "Why did you jump into such a serious decision, when you knew there was a chance it would not last?" Honestly, I did not think of it failing—even when it was failing, I did not think of it failing. I thought of it as something we had to endure, that we loved each other enough to get through it. Funny how when you look back, it seems so stupid. So many things were going on, and he was pushing and doing everything against making it work. My son said today, "He is probably happy. He has the house and he is still seeing you, yet he does not have to deal with the issues or us any longer." What wisdom that lad has. I know that, but somehow that does not seem right.

Right now, I just want some time to restore the right relationship with God. I can remember before how I sought God every day. I was growing, even though I was still making a lot of mistakes; the mistakes made me grow closer to God. I really have to get myself together, because I will not go back home at this time. (God, you know all the reasons. It's too painful to mention any details again.) I know God has fixed it because I need this time alone. I was losing sight of happiness, joy, and peace, and my emotions were a wreck. They had been like that for years. I believe it is time for me to get back on course. I have heard so many good messages in the last few days, so many encouraging words. I was so torn up about being married twice that I did not even want to think about the idea of another divorce. I was losing myself over this and certainly not making good, solid decisions for my own health and welfare.

I am not claiming another divorce, but at this point right now, it is in God's hands. I was also torn about the commitment I made to God that day. What about through thick and thin, richer or poorer, and till death do us part? Now we are separated after six years. But, I heard someone say the woman at the well had five husbands, and she was forgiven and made whole. That really made me feel better about my marriages. I thank You, Lord, for Your grace and mercy.

Well, I sit here on December 31, 2000 waiting for a new year, not alone, but with God. God, please remind me to take you everywhere I go this year, to shed all the ugliness I have carried around all my life. To do Your will, to honor You, to worship You in spirit and in truth. I love You, Lord, and I thank You for all You have done for me. Your will be done, not mine. I love You. Your daughter, Rkh

"There is no pain that heaven cannot heal."

"There is no sorrow that Jesus cannot fix."

January 2, 2001

Dear God, I am waiting for E.V. Hall to come on in about ten minutes. I have not listened to him in a long time. He has an awesome television ministry. Today was a much better day. Every day will be from now on, no matter what happens because of Jesus Christ, Your Son and what He has done for us. I know I have a long way to go, but I want to restore that right relationship back that I left five or six years ago, be obedient to You, and line my life up according to Your will. I know that I need Your help, and I cannot do this alone. I am anxiously awaiting the CDs I ordered. They will probably be here in three to four more weeks. I am rejoicing over them already. I love You, Lord God, and I thank You for Your Son that died on Calvary to save a wretch like me. Love You, and goodnight. Love, Your daughter, Rkh

January 3, 2001

Dear God, my precious God, glory to You and Your Son for saving me! There is so much to be thankful for, blessings seen and unseen. God, I felt so many emotions today. Sorrow, delight, fear, excitement, joy, anticipation, pain, and I imagine before it is over (or before you say it is over), I will feel many more. Church tomorrow night (thank God!). I am looking forward to that. Dear God, I am so thankful You saved me. Glory! Hallelujah, I am getting ready to watch Jim Hagan on TBN in about ten minutes. I know it will bless my soul. I am so excited about my soul being blessed. I am so excited about the things I know You will do for me when I submit my all to You. You are a just and faithful God, and I must be a just and faithful servant. Jesus suffered, and sometimes I feel so ridiculous thinking that I will not have to. Jesus stayed on course, and so I must stay on course. The past is the past. There is nothing I can change. I know I must suffer consequences from the past; I must accept situations as they are and go in Jesus' name. I need Your help, Lord. I cannot (nor do I desire to) go on my own again. I made a mess, Lord, and I know that You will fix my mess and build me back up. Hopefully, I will have learned and matured through this mess. I know that You are with me, that You are my rod and my staff, and that You will comfort me all the days of my life. Nothing can compare to Your peace and your joy. I am sorry for those who do not know of the goodness of the Lord. They must be willing to taste, and if they taste, they will see the goodness of the Lord. How sweet it is. Nothing compares to You.

Thank You for loving me in spite of myself. Thank You for forgiveness, and because of Your forgiveness I know I must forgive too. Lord, my issues are Your issues, and You told me to lay them down and to give them all to You. All my burdens are Yours, Lord. My life, my future, my past, my marriage, my finances, my children, my job—everything is yours. Let Your will be done in my life. Loving You wholeheartedly, Your daughter, Rkh

January 7, 2001

A new year...new things...old things are passed away. Dear God, praise Your holy name. You are truly worthy, Lord, to be given honor and glory. I love You, and thank You for saving me. I am so excited about the new job that I have been offered. I feel like all my tears and sorrow and all the things I have been through over the last few years have been accounted for. I believe that You have truly answered my prayers, opened the door, and all I have to do is to go in Jesus' name. That is it, bottom line. How long ago had I had that interview? God, You are mighty. As much as I want to save this marriage, as much as I want to be with him, I know that Your confirmation will come, Your will be done. Help me, Lord, not kick down doors You have closed, and help me walk gracefully through the doors You have opened for me. Help me to hold on to Your unchanging hands. Help me to go forth and produce fruit that will turn people to You. Help me deal with the pain of leaving, with not knowing what will happen to my marriage. He told me already that he cannot assure me of what will happen when I go. He has needs. (He still does not realize that this is not all about him.)

It is just like right before we got married. I can remember (though I cannot remember why, I can only speculate that I was having doubts) that he told me if we did not get the blood test done that day, on Friday, that he would not do it or come back again. I did it. God, I had not thought of that in a while. Now he is trying to do that again. He is trying to manipulate me again. He loves himself. I am tired of being hurt by his words and actions. He may turn to someone else, but that is okay. No, it is not. It is in God's hands. All the reasons why he wants me to stay are selfish anyway. What about me? What about my sexual needs? What should I do? I mean, we do not live together now, and he is perfectly content to just have me at his beck and call. He never wants to try to work out our issues and does not want to talk about me moving back home either. Every time I ask him about it, he says he does not want to talk about it right now. I told him that I would come back or we could work something out, but that is not good enough for him. He said he would not even consider moving either. God, please guide me, oh great Jehovah. Lead me, Lord. Take my hand, precious Lord. I love You, Lord, and I am seeking Your face and Your will and direction for my life. I know I am not perfect. Please, Lord, change me so that I may be more and more like Jesus! Thank You. I am going to church in about thirty minutes, and I cannot wait. I love You, Lord, and thank You for being who you are. Love, Your daughter, Rkh

January 13, 2001

With anything good, there is always opposition. I do believe that. My grandson brought home a Bible verse to learn today. It is. "Lo, I am with you always" (Mathew 28:20). The Bible is true; His Word is good. His Word is all we as believers have. We know in our hearts that He will always be with us, and that is why we can do all things. Even though we cannot even see our way sometimes, we continue to press on because we know that God is not a man that He shall lie. I lie because of my sinful nature, but God "is not a man that he shall lie, nor the son of man that he shall re-pent." I repent because of my sinful nature. He is just to accept our repen-tance if we will only humble ourselves.

I saw my husband today. I had a flat tire. As usual, he did not speak to me, and he seemed irritated, in a hurry, and as if I was a nuisance, off to help out at the Boys' Club again—off to the rescue and help others to show them what a great guy he is. But when it comes down to me and mine, where are the love and the compassion for us? Off to show the entire world that they can count on him, off to show "them" that matter, I suppose, that they can trust him, count on him, and that he is reliable, dependable, and supportive. How nice! How commendable! I would have loved for him to have been that way to me. Maybe it is me. I need to be by myself. Maybe I have something that turns people off, makes them defensive. Maybe I have a judgmental eye, something that makes people uncomfortable. I know I need Jesus. Jesus, I need You so bad. I do not understand at all what is going on. But then again, do I? Does it all go back to unequally yoked, or do I dare stand in judgment of my spouse? Is it me? Lord, if it is me, Lord God, I pray that You reveal it to me and cleanse me from any ugliness right now. I only tried to love him.

God renew in me a clean heart and a right spirit. Jesus, Jesus, I need You so bad. I am absolutely nothing without You. I am helpless. I know how Paul felt when he said, "We are like sheep for the slaughter." Time is winding down, and soon I will be gone. I do not know if I will ever return again, but I know that I will be gone. I do not know what the future holds out there; just know that I am going. I should be scared to death and trem-bling, but I am not—that is the Jesus in me. I am just so sorrowful that I have to leave a husband behind. I do not know what the future holds. Only

God knows. So many people will not understand because they have not walked in my shoes. They have not lived my life. Do they know that if they do not find God, they are going to lose? Don't they know that God's children have the victory? They may gain all the material wealth in the world, but they will not win in the end. Does my husband know that he is losing? I do not think he even realizes that he is losing. If only he knew that Satan will take all he has—his wife, his soul, his spirit, his zest and zeal for life, his joy, his happiness—and leave him bitter, mean, cruel, selfish, unable to get along with others, angry, and hurt, and then destroy him completely. I will pray for him always. That is why we must guard our hearts. That is what the Bible tells us to do. There is no pain that Jesus cannot fix.

My husband has turned his back on me. I am leaving, and he has turned his back. I called, and he said he was waiting for someone to come over. He said that he was going to the club Saturday night because he needed the money and on Sunday, he was working at the NCO Club. So, no time for me. He also said that we might as well get used to it because we would not be seeing each other anyway after a while. So I guess that means I have no help, no support, no nothing from him throughout my transition period. I am not surprised, just as I said before. I am not shocked or even devastated. When I made this decision, I knew he was not going to like it, support it, or stand by me. I knew he would turn his back. But God, I know that You can change anything with a twinkling of an eye. You can change a heart, a mind in a split second, if we only believe. I only ask that Your will be done. God, not mine, but Your will be done. If I suffer, it will be for righteousness' sake. God, I believe in my heart I tried. I tried so hard to make this marriage work. I suffered long and hard. I put up with a lot of things, and I sacrificed so much. I know You know all about it. I only wanted a family. I never wanted so much pain and to make such a mess of our lives. God, what am I chasing? What am I running away from? Love, Your daughter, Rkh

January 20, 2001

Well, today was just another Saturday. My daughter is back and has been since last Tuesday, January 16. I hope everything falls into place. I am sure it will. Regardless, I know that I must report to my new job on March

12, Lord willing. I do not know how I will feel leaving the city that has become so familiar to me. I will probably feel a little relieved because so much has happened here. I am sort of glad to be leaving, even if it is only for a few years. Who knows what will happen? But I am going, and I am trusting and believing in Jesus' name. I really feel sad and hurt, but not devastated. I guess I have been hurt so badly these days that I really feel numb. I am tired of crying for mankind. The tears that I cry now will be for God—hoping that Gabriel will blow that trumpet, and we will meet Jesus in the air. That is what I will be looking forward to from now on. All other things are just not important. I will just accept the things I cannot change and change the things I can. I cannot make someone understand what Jesus can do and will do for them. I do not want this marriage to end, but I cannot keep pouring my heart, mind, and soul into it. I have for six long years through tears, sorrow, pain, and so many other things that I just cannot handle it anymore. I cannot fix everything and everybody. I should have just left it alone, remained single, and went on with my life. Now I have to give up another marriage that is not mine to give up.

Marriage is the institution in which God has spoken over a man and a woman to connect them in holy matrimony unto Him. It is not mine or my spouse's institution to do with as we please. The commitment is to God. That is why it is such an important decision to make. I know that I loved him at the time, and I know that I thought I was doing the right thing, and I did my best, but I guess it was not good enough for some. I sacrificed so much, and I almost sacrificed my children. You do not know the cost of my praise. You were not there when God came and rescued me. You do not know what I went through. You don't know how God sustained and kept me…"Alabaster Box" (CeCe Winan).

Right now, I am broken, but I know my Father will be there. I know that on March 12, I will report to work and begin again—like a new start, whether I want one or not. That is the way it is. That is so familiar in my life. I have to believe and trust in God! This time, I will try to do it right. Joy river, comforter, peace that surpasses all understanding—that is who you are to me—a life-changer. I know God will redeem me and build me back up. Redemption is now!

March 31, 2001

God, I cannot believe all this time has passed, and I have not written in my beloved journal. I enjoy reading back and seeing the things God has allowed me to endure, to overcome, and understand. Well, I am at work in the Pentagon, just another face in the crowd you would think, but no. I know God has placed me here for a reason and a season. My transition was awesome, and God did it. I know He did. I neither had the strength, patience, nor the endurance to go through what I did. Thank God for Jacob, who helped me one more time. He has been a true friend to me, and I thank God for him even today. Truly, he has been a guardian angel that God placed in my life. May goodness and mercy follow him all the days of his life. We are settled in our apartment, my son and I. I miss my daughter and my grandson and also my oldest son. I miss "him," and I pray for him always. I do not know what tomorrow will bring, but I know that it will bring goodness and grace and new mercies. I know the Lord has been with me every day! I only have to believe and to reach out and touch the hem of His garment. That is all any of us have to do. He has given me so much peace and joy. Even through moving to a totally new place and a totally new job, He has kept me safe from harm. He has lifted me out of the miry clay and smiled upon me. He has put my feet upon the rock, and now I know I love You, I need You, and though my world may fall, I will never let You go. God is so good.

My transition was awesome, even down to me and my son basically moving all the furniture in our second-floor apartment alone. God gave us the strength. On my first trip to the Pentagon I got lost for two hours (one hour in D.C.) before I found my way home. Home is home, and I feel at home. I feel like I have been here a long time. I like it. Actually, I love it. I love the solitude and the dependency I have on God—how I know He will make a way out of no way. I know that in spite of all the obstacles, I am supposed to be here.

This morning, He gave me a scripture: Romans 10:12. It says, "For there is no difference between Jew and Gentile; the same Lord is Lord of all and richly blesses all who call on Him." That is awesome. That ministered to my heart. All night long, I had been praying and repenting because God told me to stop saying I was broke and that I was going to starve. I had been claiming this since I moved to the area. Lord knows it is a really high cost of living area, and I did not get a huge raise. It was okay, but not what I need to live comfortably in this area. So as a result of that, I had been saying things like, "I do not know how I am going to make it, and I need a part-time job." Well, God told me to stop speaking those negative things into my life and to stop speaking negatively about my circumstances, because every chance I had, I would almost jokingly make a comment like that. It was a standing joke with the lower-ranking federal employees in the area. God said to start calling those things that are not as though they were.

I know that is what He wanted me to do and what He wants me to do even today. After seeing how much I would bring home every other week, I sat down with some coworkers, and we were complaining about how hard it was to make it, about how high the cost of living was, etc. I jokingly even said, "I am going back home." Then, I emailed a friend of mine who had moved here about a year ago and told her I was literally going to starve to death. Last night, I felt really bad about it because I know God has called us into prosperity, and He did not bring me all this way to leave me high and dry. He has begun a good work in me, and He is just to finish the good work. I know He directed me here and has revealed to me not to speak negatively about it in any way.

All last night, even in my sleep, it seems I was repenting and praying to God about my circumstances. Even on the bus ride home, I felt His presence. This morning before I got up, I was resting, abiding in Him, feeling so much peace and joy He gave me Romans 10:12. I scrambled out of bed and got my Bible and He said again, "For there is no difference between Jew and Gentile; the same Lord is Lord of all and richly blesses all who call on Him." That is awesome. Awesome! Thank You, King of kings, Lord of lords. Thank You, provider. I love the Lord, and He heard my cry. May I always do His will and love Him all the days of my life. God, bless all my family and all the people of the world. You are a just and faithful God! Love, Rkh

April 8, 2001
Dear God, I know that You are with me always. I thank You for Your

grace and mercy and how You are always providing for me. I love You very much, and I know that my life is in Your hands. I am glad I attended Lighthouse Church of God today. Lord, please direct me and keep my family and me. Lord, help me to accept the things I cannot change, the courage to change the things I can, and the wisdom to know the difference. Lord, I need Your help in all areas of my life. Renew my mind, Lord, and help me be an overcomer of circumstances. I know that I am the apple of Your eye. You told us that in church today. Help me have wisdom and change the way I am so that I can be pleasing in Your sight. Please take care of me and prepare me to do Your will. Help me to be a good wife and mother. I love You, Lord, and I pray that I am a blessing to the people in my family, on my job, and every where I go. I just cannot say I love You enough. Love, Your daughter, Rkh

April 29, 2001

Dear God, about three weeks have passed since I have written. Things are fine because of my relationship with Jesus and the Holy Spirit inside of me. I am so thankful for this relationship that sustains me. I am not attending church this morning, but searching the channels for a good sermon. There were none. But they are showing Christian videos on the Black Entertainment Network, so I have stopped there. I cut the weave out of my hair, and I am afraid that I messed my hair up. I prayed about it first. I was tired of the hair piled on top of my head. I did not like it at all. So now, I do not know what I am going to do. I have hair issues. You know all about it. When I get to heaven, I will be perfect. That is what I wait upon. I thank You, Lord, for Your grace and Your mercy that allow me to endure all the issues of life.

I did go home for Easter weekend. It was good to be home with my family. Everyone is growing up. My spouse met me there, and we enjoyed each other. We did not talk much about our separation, but we tried to just be together. We argued, and of course he lost control of his temper, and we wasted Sunday night as usual on the edge of the bed, not together, but on opposite ends. We tried to be together, though. I never know what he is thinking and feeling; he never opens up. But when he is angry, he can definitely tell you where to go and how to get there. That is strange to me. I do not know what the future holds, but I keep hanging on to the Master's un-changing hand. That is all I have, and really that is all I need. As far as my family, I try to be a positive influence, but it just seems like it is always something hindering me. It is always the same—money issues, survival, something. I do not know, Lord, just bless us, Lord, and keep us, for You know what a feeble people we really are. The devil is a liar, and he has no victory.

Lord, as far as my marriage is concern, I am really unsure about it all. It seems so easy for my spouse to call it quits, so easy for him to go on without me. It even seems he is doing so well without me. He cooks, cleans, and does the yard. He even planted flowers we bought almost two years ago. He knows how hard I worked to try to have a flower garden. He seems content to just have the house. That seems so much more important to him than our relationship. It seems he will do nothing to try to keep our relationship together. Even last night, we talked over an hour, but not about us—just about the house, the job, and other issues (my driver's license, Memorial Day weekend, taking a trip, etc.), but never about us. He says he loves me every time we hang up. Not in a serious, "Babe, I love you" kind of way, but a "Luv ya" kind of awkward way. I know it is hard for him to open up, but that is what I want and long for. It has been two months since I left. He keeps saying, "It is in God's hands," but I do not know if he is just saying that it is destiny and what happens will happen: "Que sera, sera…Whatever will be will be…" I do not know anymore. I just pray about it and hope for the best. We need You in our life, Lord.

My spouse has this "Going to church once a month is enough" thing that he is doing now. How many phases will he go through before he gets it? "I will go to church on the first Sunday, that is all." That is only twelve times a year. I do not understand him at all. He doesn't want a relationship, and he does not want to change. He feels that he is okay just the way he is. On the other hand, I am not satisfied with the way that I am, and I really want change. I want God to make me over again, to mold me into what He wants me to be. I need You, God, to help me with me. I do not know what is going to happen. I am here, and he is there. I am not sure if we will ever live together as husband and wife again. It would be nice to work together to resolve all of our issues, and when we cannot do it we could get down on our knees and ask God for guidance.

Honestly, I never wanted to be separated from him. I moved out, and I know that was best for my son and me at the time. I also know that it was a relief for him as well. It was a major relief for me because I was dealing with all kinds of issues, trying to work full-time, going to school full-time, trying to raise children, and trying to accept the blended family. It was a first for me. It had only been me and the kids for years prior to him.

Although I moved out, I only moved about ten minutes from the house, and he wanted me to come over on the weekends. We knew we did not want to get a divorce, but we also knew that living together was too much of a stress and a lot of agony. As far as him moving to Virginia, he does not want to even talk about it. So, that is that. Where do we go from here? I do not want to go back there, and he does not want to come here. But we do not want to get a divorce. How complicated can life get? In all fairness, I guess he should not have to move here; after all, we had not agreed about me moving anyway.

I knew I had to get away at least for a while. We were arguing, and I was really hurting and torn at the same time. My career was going nowhere fast, and I did what I thought was the best for everyone. I am willing to move back home in several years if things work out. I hope they do. I want to see him Memorial Day weekend, but I will not tell him that. I won't ask or suggest it. I am going to my mother's to spend time with her and my sister. I know this sounds like "woe is me," but I love him and I want to get back together with him. But I do not want our lives together to be miserable. I want to snuggle up to him at night, and I love the idea of coming home to him and him coming home to me. I loved going out with him and just being with him. But, Lord, it is truly in Your hands. I cannot reconcile with him and return to the same conditions. When the time is right, things will fall into place if we are supposed to be together in the future. All these buts, right? But the Lord knows the answers to all things and can turn things around. I know that through all the trials and tribulations, He has not let me down one time. He worked everything out. It might not have been the way I thought it should be, but I know it was all for my good.

God will have to change both of us, and we must become more grounded and rooted in God. We both have to work on our marriage and our relationship. We get along well, but we just cannot seem to agree to disagree, and the children issues were becoming outrageous. If it were up to me, I would run home right now if I knew he had a right relationship with You. I know we both need work in that area. Some days I can be good as gold, and on others I can be just as impish as ever. Honestly, if he just asked me to come back or if he just would have said, "Don't go," I think I would have stayed. But he never said that. I would even transfer back if he asked. I do want to be with him. But there are so many issues…so many issues. That is why we have to take one day at a time and trust God and believe in God to make it through. I love You, Lord. Please keep me in perfect peace in spite of my trials and tribulations. Love, Your daughter, Rkh

Afterthought: "All things work together for the good of those who love the Lord and are the called according to his purpose."

May 12, 2001

Dear God, things are going okay, as you know. I am sure from where You sit, you know how they will go until the end. I thank You for who I am and who I am in You. Other than that, it is nothing; there is not anything else—just so many empty people, uncaring, going through the motions. But with Your people, there is so much hope! Although sometimes I feel sad, I know there is hope. That is why I wait. I would love to go out and see the city and surrounding areas, but it all seems so pointless. I know that I am married, and I know that I have to keep that commitment. I never want to live without You. I am afraid without You. I cannot breathe, move, or live without You, Lord. One thing I do know is that I do not desire to live in this world without Your love. No matter what I go through, You sustain me, hold me, console me, and keep me in peace. I love You, Lord. That is the only thing I know for sure. I know you are real, and I know You will take care of me.

I need to stop watching TV. I cry for everything—especially when it ends up good and especially love stories. I love to see couples in love, to watch them and watch how they interact with each other. There is something in their body language and actions that lets everyone know, "We are together and love each other." I often pray and hope that they can make it through all the issues of life that they may encounter. I do not know why I hope so much that they can make it through. I know all couples go through trials, but I love the ones who overcome and become closer as time goes on, probably because I have had so many sorrowful stories in my life. And these are not just in my life (I have had my share), but when I look back at my mother, sisters, my sister-in-law and others in my family, it seems so sad. That is why I pray for marriages, my friends' marriages, and the couples I come in contact with. I am going to start praying even more for marriages.

I think about being a little girl sometimes and not having a father and cannot help but think that maybe things would have been different. I cannot dwell on those things or on my past relationships and past hurt. I am who I am. My past is just that, and God knows the rest. God has brought me through all of that. My present outweighs my past. My relationship now is what I focus on. I pray to God that I make the right choices. Even though we are not together right now, nor have we lived together for seven months, I am hopeful. I know that I have to pray hard for our relationship and marriage. I have to go on to see what the end is going to be. I am excited about church tomorrow, and I will be glad to worship with all the other saints. I cannot wait to worship and sing unto my Lord, for He is worthy to be praised. He is more than worthy! Glory! Hallelujah! Love, Your daughter, Rkh

Afterthought: We are more than conquerors!

May 16, 2001

Dear God, thank You for Your grace and mercy. I always need You every minute of the day. The devil is a big fat liar—the things he tries to make me believe. I believe what Your Word says, and it tells me that I am more than a conqueror through Your Son Jesus Christ. "I am the head and not the tail; above and not beneath; I am blessed coming in and going out!" That is the report that I will believe. Thank You, Lord, for everything—for my job, my apartment, my health, my strength, my mother, my family, my friends, and for the Holy Spirit that keeps me in my right mind. I pray today and every day Your will be done in my life. I have messed up my life long enough. God, You know my needs and wants, my desires, my concerns and You care about the smallest detail in my life. I hear You whispering, "Rest my child, enjoy this time of relaxation. For part-time work and school will come."

Lord, I want so many things to happen. Lord, only allow the things You have for me to happen. No matter what it is and no matter how I pray, You know what is best for me. Help me pray wisely and unselfishly to You. Give me wisdom at home, at work, and everywhere I go. I love You, Lord. I dedicate my life to You. There is no pain that Jesus cannot fix. I know this will help me keep my focus on what is important and continue to focus on You and serve You the best way I know how. I do not have to go into details. You know my thoughts today, earlier, and every day. Let Your will be done, Lord. Teach me, Master, teach me. Teach me how to pray and to walk in Your love. Love, your daughter Rkh

No Date
Dear God, I woke up early this morning without the alarm clock going off. I was thinking and going over "me." As much as I say I believe and trust in You, my actions are totally the opposite. I screamed at my son today when he came home. I hit him a couple times for coming in later than he should. It was dark on a Wednesday night, and he acts like school is the last thing on his mind. Then I heard he was at a friend's house out of the neighborhood, and that made me mad. He knows that is against the rules totally. Something is very wrong. I am reading a book on walking in love and the beatitudes: love, peace, kindness, gentleness, etc., and I am acting the total opposite. That is the way I act. I do not pick up my Bible like I know I should. I lay around and watch TV every evening and fuss at my son about the things he is not doing. He is not doing what he should. He is not holding up his end of the bargain, like cleaning, responsibility, his homework, etc. I am not fulfilling my obligations either. I am not tithing, not reading the Word, not praying as much as I should. I try to read. (I have a lot of books to read, but I have not read one yet.) I did read one, but I had to start over. When we read books, we should change into what we have read or at least apply it to our lives. As much as I love God and write in this book, faith without works is dead. There are so many issues going on. I do not know if I am depressed or what. My issues are my spouse, my son, school, and needing a part-time job, studying Your Word, what church to go to, and adjusting to a new job and a new city.

My job is just another paycheck, my apartment so expensive, and relocating has caused so many new adjustments in my life. I am not doubting, but maybe I am deep within, because my actions certainly say the opposite. I am doubting myself, doubting God, doubting my spouse, doubting our relationship, doubting my son, doubting my decision to relocate, doubting everything. All these things are hanging over my head, even the "vacation." Maybe I should not go. I do not know. I need You, Lord, to help me walk in Your love. I cannot do it alone. What is wrong with me? Am I pushing everybody away? I know my son is thinking, "My mother is supposed to be a Christian, but she is so mean." I do not feel the love and peace I need. Maybe I need to drop these heavy loads I thought I had given to God. But I keep carrying the heaviness.

I called my husband at least six times today. It just seems like I am waiting to hear him tell me something. What I am waiting to hear, I do not know. Two more issues are our relationship and the children. What are we going to do? We were together and could not get it together. We had it all, but we were not in Christ together. Our issues are still there, and him coming will not change the fact that we could not live together peacefully. Teach me how to act. It seems that I can talk a good talk, that I can write of my love, but God, I need to walk that walk also. I need to demonstrate that love. Lord, I pray that You will teach me and give me wisdom and help me conquer all my fears. Help me to be obedient, stay on my budget, have a loving disposition, and work hard in my job. You know, Lord, and You are so awesome. I thought after I got a new job, new start, and new residence and left all that other stuff behind, I would be fine, but in my spirit I feel unsatisfied, unproductive, and almost lost. If it were not for my knowledge of Your Word, I do not think I would make it.

Through it all, there is one thing I know, and that is God's sustaining words. We cannot base anything on our feelings. We must base everything on God's spoken Word (the Bible). I feel awful. I feel like I am trying to do it myself. I know I need to let go and listen to God's direction. My heart is saying "Yes, Lord," but it seems that I am afraid, that I am scared that if I let go of everything, the result will be disastrous. Feelings! I need to start right now, Lord, and get a handle on my life right now. I beg You every minute to help me or I will make so many more mistakes. Help me decrease and You increase in me. Oh, Lord, I need Thee. Without You, I am nothing, and with You, I am everything. I do not want to just wear a smile, I want to *be* a smile, be the sunshine, be a comforter, be a kind and gentle person who is loving and caring to all people. Give me strength.

May 19, 2001

It is four a.m. Lord, give me the strength to be what You would have me to be. Not loud (if I ever was), not wisecracking, unfriendly, or snobbish, but peaceful, humble, quiet and hard-working. I love You, Lord, and I dedicate myself to You. I do not understand why it is such a struggle because I love You so much. You are my life, and You are the head of my life. That is why it is so hard for me to understand what is going on. I should have gone to the altar call Sunday and been renewed—who more than me needs to be renewed? But there I stood, stubborn. That was just pride. Pride comes before a fall. My Lord does not like pride, selfishness, and deceit. Am I deceiving myself? Am I talking the talk but not walking the walk? Love, Your daughter, Rkh

No Date

Dear God, my oldest son was here, and I thank you for bringing him safely to his mom one more time. Things are okay, I guess. I cannot fall to pieces every time things do not go like I would like them to, now can I? I can only go to the Father so He can strengthen me so I may continue to press on to the high calling in Christ Jesus. Lord, thank You for revelation and Your Word. Your words for me are to watch, pray, and live holy every day. Lord, I need a breakthrough. I can feel a change coming on, a good change in me. I am seeking God for answers, wisdom, and I know my breakthrough is going to come. I know it won't be long. Lord, I pray that Your will be done in my life. I pray for strength, Lord, to be an overcomer in life. The harder life gets, the more we overcome, and God takes us from glory to glory to glory. I pray that the Holy Spirit will quicken me and compel me to do what is right. I am looking heavily to this. I need to walk in the Spirit, not walk in the flesh. That is what I have done all my life, and it is time for a change, a major change. It is time for me to *change* and leave all that trouble, hurt, and pain behind me and walk in the wondrous newness of God. It is all I want to do. Holy Spirit, love me, teach me, walk with me, give me the answers, the questions, the knowledge, and the courage to walk by faith and not by what I see. God has called us to the marvelous light, and we must walk in it each and every minute. Thank You, Lord! Love, Your daughter, Rkh

June 14, 2001
God is good all the time!

July 15, 2001
Dear God, we are on vacation. I love you very much. I cannot see how people live without you at all. I need You every minute just to keep me sane. I look to my spouse for love, and he just turns away. Have I hurt him that much? Why doesn't he just end the relationship? He still continues to pursue the relationship every time he gets ready. I look for him. I search his eyes constantly and find no compassion, no love, just darkness, and I feel sad. Although I know he loves me (or I guess he loves me), I would love to see it in his eyes. The eyes are the mirror to the soul. I cannot figure us or our connection out. When he touches me or looks my way, I feel goose bumps. I love him very much. I wish he would reciprocate that love. Maybe he just does not know how. I cannot understand why he will not allow himself to let go and allow You to come into his heart. The only sign that he cares is that he remembers everything about me. He has my picture and our picture over his bed and on the wall right by the TV. I know he looks at it a lot. He still has us in the living room. That says a lot. He is also always available for me at any time. Lord, why can't I feel the love though? Even though I know that he cares, why can't I feel it? Is something so terribly wrong with me? Am I just that insecure?

July 17, 2001
Here I sit, Lord, at the Ramada Inn in Fort Lauderdale, Florida. I had my nails done. It is my favorite thing to do since my hair right now has seemingly no hope. God is a miracle worker. My hair definitely needs a miracle. I have learned over my lifetime not to think negatively. I look over my life and I wonder why some of the things have happened, and I realize that that is who I am. God made me, God knew me, and when He finishes

with me, I will shine like pure gold. (I am looking forward to that). God, You have your work cut out for You. But, You are a miracle worker. Give me confidence in who I am, and help me treat everyone with love and kindness and respect. Help me do the things You would have me to do and order my steps. I love You, Lord, and I dedicate my life to You. Help me not take advantage or take for granted the opportunities You have allowed me. I love You, God, and I thank You for being here for me and for having the Holy Spirit guide me. Sincerely, Rkh

Afterthought: Thank You for today.

July 18, 2001

Here I am on a cruise ship going to Nassau, Bahamas, for the second time. How blessed am I? I ask God for protection and thank Him immensely. I am sitting here sipping a cup of coffee, so aware of your presence. God, I do not know where I would be without You. I feel lost in the flesh, but in my spirit, I do not. That is why your Word says, "Walk in the spirit." I have been walking in the flesh a lot lately. This vacation has been okay, but we have not really talked about our issues or what our plans are. It is hard. I would have enjoyed it a lot better if my son had come. I need to take him somewhere, too, and let him know no matter what that I always love him. It is hard, God, and I know You know this; You know my struggles daily. My spouse is so hard to love. I really do not believe he loves me, and right now I do not need it like I used to and that is sad. I am at the point that either you love me or you do not. All that matters is that I know that no matter how I act, God loves me, and that is more precious than anything to me.

It is hard, God, and I know You know this; You know my daily struggles. I have never been through such in my life. Lord, I just want to go back home. I have no idea where this marriage will end up. Why take a vacation if you are miserable and you are making everyone else miserable? This is so sickening. I wonder why I hang on. It is obvious he does not want my help or my love, and he can do without me. It is obvious I can do without him also. It is obvious he has everything under control (yeah, right). We do not live together now anyway. He pays his bills, and I pay my own. We live in two totally different states. There are so many issues. He is so unhappy, and

I believe he has really given up. He does not know how he can be happy with Jesus. I continue to search his eyes for a sparkle or glimmer of hope, and I see nothing. Just emptiness.

Maybe I make him sad; maybe it is me. I moved out. I moved away, and still nothing has changed. As time goes by, I feel like we just do not have a chance unless God intervenes in our situation on both our behalves. I know I am not perfect either. But I do try. I am a very balanced person and certainly not insecure or needy. I just need what I need at times, and that is the essence of who I am as a woman. If it does not work with him, then I know I will probably never get married again and I will live by myself for a very long time. Funny, but I really did believe that we were meant to be together. I cannot imagine myself with anyone else. Of all the people I have met in my life, there has not been anyone like him. However, as badly as I want it to work, I know that right now it is best for us to live apart.

There is something so unhealthy about our relationship. As good as it gets, the bad times are as bad as it can get. When we were together, we made each other miserable. We were always arguing about something, and he was actually unkind, cruel, and so selfish at times. I am sorry if it seems as if I am just being judgmental, but it is the truth, and I had to get this off my chest and to spend some intimate time with You, Lord. I know this sounds like a gripe session, but I need to vent right now. I can tell You everything and can pour out all of my frustrations and anxieties on You, and You will not judge me. You will only listen and restore. I know I am not much in the world's eyes, but I look at myself as You see me. You see me as more than a conqueror; You see me as an over comer; You see me as precious and fearfully and wonderfully made. I am secure in You and You only.

As I look back, I know that in some ways a lot of people did not believe in me, but through You and my relationship with You, I know that I can believe in myself. I know You have so many things to show me and so many things for me to do. Thank You, Lord God. Your daughter, Rkh

July 19, 2001

It is raining in the Bahamas. It is around five p.m. The day was okay. I read and thought and thought and read. My husband and I are not really talking right now. I just want to go home where there is peace and I can get back to my jobs, to my life as I know it now. I did not leave the ship today as I had planned. I planned to do nothing really, and nothing really happened like I planned. My husband again did without me, and I did without him as well. I could not help but think that we really are doing the right thing by living apart. Sometimes I think that we should part ways completely with no hard feelings. I look back, and there is so much pain and anxiety in the beginning, and even today. Maybe I bring out the worst in him. I do not know. Sometimes I wonder. I really believe that it is over for us; at least that is how I feel today. I want it over and I am tired of the games. But, I know that I cannot rely on my feelings. I may feel totally different tomorrow. How can we fix such pain inflicted on each other? We really should have left well enough alone, and I should have remained single. I certainly was not ready for what I got. I thought it would be different. We are so different, and we have different views in life, about life, and about love. We also have a different view of God and being a Christian. He does not care about the things of God. I was definitely not thinking that we would have problems with that. We attended church faithfully, and I was hoping that after listening to so much of God's Word, there would definitely be a change in both of us. I know that I need to change, and I am open for any change that I need to make. My spouse is so closed-minded and not open for any change, even if it means losing his wife. He just does not want to change, and he refuses to improve himself or his actions. He always says, "I am me, and I change not." I laugh because that is what God said, "I am God, and I change not." But God is perfect and does not need to change. As humans, we need to be transformed. Change is inevitable for us because we have to shed our sinful nature in order to please God. We cannot do that unless we embrace change. God is always working on us and compels us to change so that we can be pleasing in his sight. We all need change, and we should always be open to positive change and spiritual development. Change is what will help enhance our relationships and help us to become better people.

I can only say, God, I am sorry for all the wrong I have done and all the things I did that were not right. I am sorry for all the things I said and did to make this marriage so messed up. I know I have at times been very ugly to my husband and that I have contributed to all the problems we are having. I am sometimes selfish and unreasonable. Sometimes, I can be so mean. But I can say that I have changed so much in the last few years. I am a lot more patient and understanding these days. Through all the experiences, trials, and tribulations, I know that God has been working on me. I feel His presence in spite of any circumstances. Though I feel so helpless being here, and instead of enjoying myself, I am laying in this room full of regret. But through it all, I know that I am trusting God for wisdom and courage to keep pressing on. I feel His peace in the midst of this storm. I know that I can pray and pour my heart out, and He will listen and comfort me. Although I may falter in many of my ways, I know that I love God, and He has brought me a long way. I wish I could go back and change all the mess, but I know that is impossible. Lord, forgive me for all the wrong that I have done and please, Lord, bless my husband. It is hard because he is just inches away with his same old attitude and non-caring self. I can just feel the attitude, and it is overwhelming me.

Tomorrow is another day, and soon I will be on my way. I will say goodbye, and I will make amends, but as far as pushing this relationship or trying to work it out, I will just back off and go on with my life and put my marriage in Your hands. Lord, give me strength. Rkh

September 11, 2001

On this very sad day in history, I look toward heaven but never ask why. I wonder why I never asked why. It is so strange, because deep down inside, I know why. But I lack the wisdom at this time to articulate the why of September 11. Some day, we will all understand, but I hope right now that something I might say or have said will make millions understand just a little bit better. Today, I just grieve. I grieve for the people who died. I grieve for the loss, grieve for the people who did this, and grieve because there are people so lost that they are capable of such a thing. I grieve because of the feeling of helplessness, grieve because I am so far away from home, grieve for all the families who lost husbands and wives, sisters and brothers, aunts and uncles, cousins, sons and daughters, mothers and fathers and friends, coworkers and acquaintances. There is so much loss and so much hatred—evil at its finest. To see evil and experience evil, to be a part of such an evil act does something inside of you. It stirs up so many emotions inside, emotions you never thought you had. It makes you realize and appreciate life. It allows you to come to the realization that the world is not perfect and that the world is certainly not in control of matters. It shows how vulnerable we all are. We think we are on top, yet we are not. We think we have it all together, but we do not. We are like sheep for the slaughter. I am not afraid...just very sad inside to know how vulnerable we all are.

September 11 was the day I experienced the ultimate life-changing experience. I think I experienced every emotion imaginable that day. I have experienced a lot along the years, as my journey has revealed, but September 11 was a day that I will never ever forget because I was there. That day touched everyone in some way or another, but for me it not only made me realize what living was all about, it introduced me to my God all over again, this time in a different capacity. It allowed me to experience His awesomeness at a whole new level. Why I was there at the Pentagon that day or even working at the Pentagon had always been a mystery to me. I wondered and thought about it time and time again. I never set out to work there or even planned it. It happened in the midst of my struggles. I was struggling with a lot of things: a dead-end job, a marriage that seemed so right but was so rocky, and a major decision on what I wanted to do and become. I was so close to graduating with a BS degree with a major in accounting. I had worked so hard and literally struggled to maintain a good GPA. I admit some of the courses were very challenging, and if it weren't for a few good classmates, I would have been in trouble. But I made it and was getting very close to graduating. At this very exciting time in my life, it took ten long years of going to school part-time, raising three children, and working full-time to obtain such a feat. Time was drawing near, and I was terribly excited. That was definitely a motivating factor in my life. Funny that I never even thought about making more money or obtaining a degree for my own advancement or material gain. I was just so pleased to have been able to achieve something that took so much time, so much hard work, and so much sacrifice. Although this was a pivotal point in my life, that was about the only thing I had going for me other than God.

My marriage was very rocky, and my career was stagnant. I worked hard, but it seemed like I was always in someone else's shadow. My hard work and dedication was not appreciated. This was proven by management when they had a chance to promote me and passed me up and brought someone from overseas to fill the vacant position in our office. I often wondered why, but I guess I know the why of that as well. I was only four courses shy of my accounting degree, and management knew this but for some reason decided to select another individual. I was hurt, but not devastated. Like I said, I know the why of it. That was the last straw, or shall I say the barrel that broke the monkey's back. I sat down and pondered over my own life, not what someone had done or not done, not the "somebody done somebody wrong" of it, not the "someone owes me," but the "what in the world am I going to do now?" kind of pondering. This kind of pondering has always resulted in significant change in my life. When I am truly open, truly honest about me, myself, and I, this is when I thoroughly exam myself and make some major decisions in my life. I only concentrate on what I have done, what I can do, and how I can change me—just me and no one else. That is what I did. I summed it up by saying, "My marriage is messed up and I cannot fix it. My job is messed up, and I cannot change anyone's mentality, and I am not helping the situation by complaining, crying, kicking, or blaming anyone." I knew that I had to fix me. I knew that I had some tough decisions to make. I decided that at this point, it was pointless to focus on my marriage. I had prayed for so long for a breakthrough, and it just had not come. I decided to concentrate on my career—on something I *could* change (like the wise Serenity Prayer). I decided to leave and to pursue some goals for myself that would help me in the long run and to leave all this behind me and find a new job. I really did not know much about finding a new job in another state, but I soon found out and began to apply. I was determined that if this was what God wanted to do in my life, He would lead me in the right direction and open up the door He wanted me to walk through.

I did speak to my spouse (we were separated at the time, living apart), and he said that he understood and if that is what I wanted to do, then he would not try to stop me. I did not want to hear that response. I actually wanted to hear, "Baby, please don't go!" but he did not say that, and so I continued my quest. I knew so little about any other state other than the one I was born and raised in. I just kept praying. I received rejection after rejection, but I was determined. Finally, I had a phone call, a telephone interview, and a start date with promotion potential. My emotions were running wild. Fear, excitement, and doubt crowded my mind. What would I do? How would I get there? Would I be able to do the job well? Where would I stay, and what would people say, especially my spouse whom I was still seeing on a regular basis?

Since 1992, I always went to God and prayed about everything. So I prayed and prayed some more. Although I accepted the job immediately, it took time to finally find some resolve within me. I did not make the final decision to actually move and report there for about a month. My report date was on March 12, 2001 at the Pentagon. I had never been to that area, and just the thought of working there made me tremble, first with fear and then with excitement. My spouse was upset, and my family did not understand at all. I did not understand the why of it. I had to go. That is all I knew. I had to go.

At the time, I was completing three of the last four courses I needed to graduate and had made an agreement with the Personnel Office to relocate to northern Virginia after I finished the three courses. Although I know that something compelled me to go, I still had reservations about my marriage. I was so glad to leave my current position and to get a long awaited promotion. I was excited about the opportunity to work somewhere else and remain in the Federal Government. By that time, I had fifteen years with the Feds, and I did not want to give that up. But I wanted my marriage to work. I think we both did, but now this. By then, my mind was made up, and my spouse agreed that I should go, although I knew he was very angry and upset about me leaving. He, just like me, thought after I left, the marriage would be over. We still saw each other up until the very last night I was there, and then we said goodbye, not knowing what would happen. He even said, "You know, if you leave, it will probably be over for us." I said, "I know." As bad as it hurt, I knew I had to go. I did not know every aspect of it, but I knew that I had to do this.

During the three months I prepared to move and prepared to finish the three courses, a lot of things happened. First, I did not graduate. I was going through so much in my marriage. I was busy trying to maintain a relationship with my spouse and being depressed about us not living together, being depressed because I would be leaving soon, and being stressed about relocating to an unfamiliar huge city and wondering if I could fit the bill at the Pentagon and being alone in a strange city. Ultimately, I dropped two of the three classes I needed. I was also going through a lot at work. It seemed that once my managers and coworkers found out I was leaving, they became very hard to deal with. I was basically sat in a corner to do nothing as punishment for leaving. That was hard because I did not want to leave on bad terms.

I was praying to God all the time to please give me some confirmation that what I was doing was what He wanted for my life. It did not come easy, and only after I was almost ready to change my mind, confirmation came. Thank You, Jesus! It came from a classmate that I did not know at all. We were in the same classroom for weeks, and we only acknowledged each other in class. But one particular night, we were thrown together to do a group project. We instantly began to talk about God and enjoy each other's wisdom in Christ. She was a very spiritual person and even seemed to be on a whole different level than I was. She knew the Word, and I enjoyed talking to her. I looked forward to talking to her each night. We shared a lot. I cannot remember if I shared everything, but we both bonded because we were sisters in Christ. I told her about my move and all the circumstances surrounding the move. I told her I was trusting God and that was the only way I was making it these days. At the time, I did not know she would be my confirmation. But she was.

One night when we were almost finished with our course, she came in and handed me a slip of paper. On the paper were scriptures. I read them after I got in my car, and I wept. That was my confirmation, and I truly prepared to leave after that. I lost contact with Yolanda after a few telephone conversations, but I read those scriptures daily. She was my confirmation, my angel, and I wish I could tell her that, but I believe she already knows. But I would welcome the chance to tell her and thank her. Angels know who they are and know their mission and when it is accomplished. That is why I believe she slipped in and out of my life the way she did. I will never forget her. This is what she gave me: Watch and pray, live holy everyday. Mark: 32-37; Acts: 20:31; Luke 21:34-36; Matthew 26:40.

On a simple torn half-sheet of paper, nothing fancy, my confirmation came. I still have the paper today, but it is wrinkled and worn. She said, "Go in peace," and I went shortly afterwards. I only spoke to her a few times after, and I think I saw her at church once right before I left.

I took her wisdom and carried it with me. That is all I needed, and it came from a perfect stranger that was sent by God. I read those scriptures every day—every morning and sometimes at night. I knew they carried me through the smooth transition of relocating and a very welcoming group of coworkers and a very special friend who was there and was always there (who is still a friend today after eighteen years) and never asked for anything except an opportunity to have Chinese food with me under an old oak tree when I am in town. Thank you. You are another friend from God, and you know who you are. I woke up every morning at four a.m. to pray and to quote those precious scriptures that meant the world to me. That is how I survived a huge change in my life. The change was good, but I still had the issue with my marriage. Some days were good, and some were not as far as my marriage was concerned. The job God placed me in was wonderful, and I fit right in. I prayed so hard prior to going there that this would be God's will and where He wanted me to be. I was convinced.

I did the best I could as far as the marriage and trying to maintain a long-distance relationship. We met as often as we could. We flew to see each other, we drove to meet each other at half way points, and we talked on the phone every day. It was obvious that our marriage would be okay and that we would survive. My spouse visited but did not like the area and would not consider moving at all. Although that is what I wanted to happen, I accepted his decision and continued to live the best I knew how. Since my husband had a definite rebellious spirit in many things, I don't know why I expected anything different. There was no reason why he could not or would not. His rationalization was simply, "I just don't want to move."

I continued to press on and read my Bible and read those scriptures every morning at four a.m., then pray, shower, and commute to the Pentagon. I did not dare to drive; the traffic was overwhelming to me. On the morning of September 11, I woke up at my usual time (four a.m.) and began to pray. I had been anointed with the gift of speaking in tongues a year or so before and spoke in tongues on occasion. But that particular morning when I began to pray, I immediately started speaking in tongues. I spoke loudly, passionately, and uncontrollably with fervor unlike any other time that I remember. I could not stop, and I spoke in tongues throughout the entire prayer. I do not remember saying anything in my own native tongue. I remember saying "I am going to fast today." I did not know quite what to think about what had just happened. I remember calling out the names of each one of my coworkers in my office. I had been at the Pentagon six months, and we had become a very close-knit team. I showered and ran out to catch the Metro bus and was on my way. During the bus ride, my mind kept wondering back to my prayer and the intensity of it. My spirit was not troubled, but my mind kept reflecting back to my morning prayer and how uncontrollably I had prayed. I kept wondering what my prayer was all about. I knew there was a reason for my prayer, but I was not afraid. I was more curious than anything. I wanted to know what it all meant.

I arrived at the Pentagon about forty-five minutes later, got off the bus, and proceeded to go up the escalator. I had a routine that I did every morning: go get Starbucks, some eggs and grits or fruit. I would get in the office about twenty minutes prior to the beginning of my workday so I had time to drink my coffee and eat my breakfast. As I was going up the escalators to enter the building at about seven-ten a.m., I got a whiff of someone's coffee, and it smelled so good. My spirit quickened instantaneously, and I remembered that I was going to fast today. I skipped the coffee and breakfast and went straight to my desk and began to work. Around seven-thirty a.m., one of our accountants came up to see my boss. She stuck her head in everyone's cubicle and gave a huge smile and a hearty good morning. The day was like any other day, or so I thought. The only thing different was that intense prayer that kept coming to my mind. "What was that all about," I wondered again.

Around eight a.m., my supervisor came around to my cubicle and mumbled something about some airplanes going off-course and not being able to track their whereabouts. We all thought, *hijacked planes*. Shortly after, we heard about the airplane that crashed into the North Tower of the

World Trade Center. The day was starting to unfold. We turned on the radio to a station in New York, and the radio announcer, clearly in tears, was describing what had just happened. She was audibly crying but still reporting the news. As we listened in bewilderment, a nation in shock, a second plane hit the South Tower. The announcer burst into tears and said, "Another plane has hit the South Tower, and clearly this is not an accident—this is an act of terrorism." We all huddled together, each person dealing with the news in their own unique way. I looked around at my newfound coworkers and friends who had welcomed me so graciously. Little did I know that we would carry a common bond forever. I called my husband, and we talked about what was going on until my supervisor called a meeting, as it was fiscal year-end close for the Army, and we were very busy. She said, "Business as usual" and that we needed to discuss overtime hours through the remainder of September.

We were all in her office when the plane hit the Pentagon. We heard and felt the impact. A couple of people ducked under a desk. The rest of us just stared at each other for a split second. There were major renovations going on in the Pentagon, and for a brief moment, we all thought it might have been some construction until we saw falling debris and smoke. We all ran. I ran to get my purse but did not put down the folders I had in my hand. It seemed everyone paired off with someone. We headed toward Center Court, but a very keen security person yelled "No! Not Center Court! We could get trapped there!" So we all split up in pairs and went in different directions. Joyce and I headed toward E-ring at first, not knowing where to go, but a group of tourists and their tour guides were running from that direction and yelled for us to turn around. I can only remember the shock on their faces and the fear of "Why today?" It was different for them than for me. We were *supposed* to be here—we came here Monday through Friday to work for the Department of Defense. I often think of them, though I do not know any one of them. But for them, they were merely taking a two-hour tour (at most) on a designated day.

At first, I thought I would fall to pieces, but I began to pray and then I remember being totally under the control of the Holy Spirit, totally submitted to Him and totally in His mercy. I did not panic. I merely began to call on Him, not because I was afraid, but because I understood what God had prepared me for and that He used me that morning to pray for protection over thousands and thousands of lives in the Pentagon and also in New York City. Glory to God! God was ultimately in control. I began to call His name and ask for mercy. I remember several people asking me if I was okay. We finally got out of the building and were about to get on the Metro train. As we proceeded to get on the train, an announcement came over the loudspeaker saying that there was an attack on the Pentagon and that the train had shut down. We stood for a second and then headed for the escalator that led to the outside of the building. No one knew at that time if there would be more planes or if it was safe being out in the open, but we all stood staring in disbelief at the building. We were all there transfixed on what we saw coming from the building—the darkest cloud of smoke, a huge cloud of smoke, coming from our place of employment. To most of us, it had become just another building that we entered and exited Monday through Friday and occasionally on the weekends. It was surreal. But it was happening; it was evil at its finest. It was a plot to kill as many people as possible, and we were a part of it.

I continued to pray for those who I knew were working on that side of the building. I also knew that in just three weeks, we were scheduled to move into the area where the plane had crashed. I also knew that our accountants could have possibly been affected. I prayed hard and just did not want to believe that anyone got hurt. But in reality, I knew it was impossible that no one would be affected. It appeared in my mind that the entire building was burning and that it would burn forever. I was forgetting what a massive structure the building was.

I remember my first day of work and how huge it was to me and how confusing it was to get from point A to point B. But at this time, it did not dawn on me because the building had become all too familiar to me, and as the days went by, the size did not even occur to me anymore. What happened was a truth that I would not come to terms with for days.

One of my friends saw a group of people who were praying and she said, "Come on, let's go pray with them," and we did. I remember later thinking of that and thinking of the irony of that, as I was always telling her to pray and seek God. As everyone stood there looking at the deep, dark black cloud of smoke coming from the Pentagon, our hearts went out to those who might have been killed inside the building. Although we were not sure what had happened, we all speculated that a plane had crashed into the building just like in New York. The question was, were we safe standing out in the open? Would there be other planes? The reality of it hit everyone seemingly at the same time, and we all scurried into cars that were leaving the area. No one knew anyone, and it did not matter. People were just stopping and picking up anyone who was in need of a ride out of the danger zone.

An ex-coworker and friend told me Yolanda called the day after the attack on the Pentagon. But during that time, everything was so hectic I do not remember if I got her number or wrote it down and lost it. We moved from the Pentagon days after the attack.

September 16, 2001

Five days after September 11, 2001. I actually wrote down the title of my book, as it is today (June 17, 2007), and I also wrote my dedications, and both will remain as it was written almost six years ago and as it will be when this book is published.

The aftermath left devastation to all. When I got home, I watched TV nonstop for days except for a couple of hours of sleep each night. I watched one of my coworker's spouse on television, waiting to hear if her spouse was dead or alive. She had so much hope. I heard all the details. I heard the names of the victims over and over again. Our office had to move out of the Pentagon because we had so much smoke and water damage. We all entered the building with heavy hearts and sadness and packed what we could salvage. "Work must go on," they said, and it did. We packed with the bodies still in the building three days later. I attended the memorials as the days passed. So many memorials. It was unreal, surreal. God bless America!

April 21, 2003
God where did the time go?

April 22, 2003
Today is my baby sister's birthday. She would have been thirty-nine

years old. May she rest in peace. I love you, Phyllis! I cannot sleep. I was very tired last night and went to sleep around nine. Well, it has been a long while. My life has changed drastically. I am no longer in Virginia working at the Pentagon. I have relocated back to Georgia. "I am just holding on to my faith"...thank you, 97.5 FM in Atlanta, Georgia. Most nights, that is the only thing that soothes my soul. I listen while I am asleep, and hopefully all that goodness is building and seeping into my mind, heart, and spirit while I rest. I have changed a lot and been through even more, but I am still here and still thanking God.

I like my job and will not complain because I prayed so hard to find a job here close to my spouse and what I was familiar with. Our relationship has not changed much. I am just able to handle things better. I love Jesus all the more because I can see how much I depend on Him for stability, and He has sustained me through everything I have been through. I can see what He has brought me out of. I have erred in a lot of ways, but He has sustained me. I have one more class to go before I graduate. It has been rough, and nobody knows but God. It has been rough raising a teenage male alone. It has taken more than I ever expected, but I know he is blessed because of me. He is blessed and highly favored just like me because of our Lord God.

Throughout all the pain, the main thing is Jesus, and that is all. As long as I keep things in perspective, I am fine. I am happy and have peace. Although I wish I could change circumstances, I know that I fly high above my circumstances and look down on them with Jesus, and even though they make me cry, I know that all is well with my soul and that is what matters most. I know Jesus suffered and died, and I know it was for all who believe in Him. He is my life! He is my joy, my hope for tomorrow.

Happy birthday, Phyllis. I know you are happy now, and tell our brother I love him and I miss him too. Even though I do not speak of either of you that often, I know what both of you meant to me, and I know that I missed so much in my life because you both left us prematurely, too early in your lives. God knows best for everyone and does not make mistakes. All of us err as humans, and God still blesses us regardless of what we do (through His grace and mercy).

Well, the highlight of my days these days is my little grandbaby. He does not even know how he blesses me, and I love him dearly. God, may goodness and mercy follow him everywhere he goes. He told me on Saturday April 19, "Grandma, I am so glad to be your grandchild." Out of the mouths of babes.

My spouse is still running and still not ready and still in denial. I wonder if he will always be that way. We are still living apart, and I am trying to deal with all the changes—the job change, relocation, and the possible fact that maybe we will never live together unless God put us back together. We are going through struggles, but that is normal I suppose. I guess the stress of two jobs in three years and moving again is getting to me. I am just trying to let go and let God. He knows what is best, and when and if the time comes, He will bring us to the places we need to be. I am still hoping that my spouse will one day just submit his will to God and cry out, "I yield, I yield." So for now, I just live here in Neward and try to do the best I can until the appointed time. To God be the glory! (12:57 a.m.) Rkh

April 27, 2003

Today, like every day, was a struggle—not like a tug of war, but just like a choice of what to think about, the joy in the Lord or the pain of life's issues. I am not in pain or hurting because I choose not to be. My mind keeps wondering back to yesteryear, to yesterday, and I know I cannot go back there. I know I cannot change anything, and I know there is no need to keep going back, yet I do. I did all I could do, said all I could say, loved all I could love, and now I am at the point that I just have to let go. Let God. It is so hard to conceive of a marriage being wrong or that you gave it your all and now there is nothing else to give. You know you still love that person, but the well is dry. It is empty, and you know that it is all up to them now and if they do not give, love, or try to make your well full again, you will never be able to put out again.

I am at the point that I even see myself without that person, see myself going on my own—not afraid, not dreading, but planning. I think of buying a house of my own. I am tired of paying rent. I have been paying rent for almost three years now. It seems pointless. I see myself alone, although I hate to see that, but it seems so much more reasonable than living like I have been. It is like a numb feeling. I can visualize it, but cannot conceive of it. But it seems so much more realistic. Things cannot keep going on like this. We are separated, living apart, and just seeing each other occasionally on the weekends. He is working on most weekends.

We are working in two different cities and living one hour away from each other. Although we talk of buying a house midway, it probably will never happen. Would we be happy living in the same house this time, or would we be miserable living together again? Would he be the loving husband, appreciative and kind? He was not before. I know he is waiting for things to change so that we can try again. But could I ever be comfortable living with him? I do not see where he has changed. I have changed. I have experienced some life-changing situations, and I have totally put all my trust in God. I am so much wiser and realize that sometimes you just might have to walk away if you cannot find peace. I have learned that no matter what obstacle we may face, God will always be there, and loss does not necessarily mean failure. It means we are human and that we need a savior. I should forgive, and I have, but do I have to do what he was not willing to do for me? We have not spoken in days. The same-old, same-old, nothing ventured, nothing gained.

I know there are worst things than being alone, and that is being somewhere where it is hell to live. Been there, done that. If someone really loved you, wouldn't they just love you regardless and make the sacrifices necessary to make the marriage work? I mean the "I do not want to drive an hour every day to and from work" thing seems lame, considering all that I have sacrificed. Yet I would do it to reap the benefit of being together. I moved hundreds of miles back and gave up promotions, etc. Does he think *that* was an easy decision? I have to stop wishing things were different, but they are not, and I just have to accept them the way they are. God knows what is best for me, and right now I am living alone because that is what is best for me and for my situation. God knows best. Everything is in his timing, and I thank Him each day for knowing because I certainly do not know. Your will, God, not mine. Thank You for a beautiful day, church, eternity, a nice dinner, and time with my son! I love You, Lord God! Your daughter, Rkh

May 26, 2003

My Father, thank You for bringing me back home safely. Thank You for watching over my son as well. Lord God, here I am again right back in the same hard place I was last month. Memorial Day and another holiday wasted for me; nothing ventured, nothing gained once again. I wish, I wish, I wish! But wishes do not change situations. Only people can change situations, yet this situation stays the same. I just take a deep breath and know that You are God and resolve that You know what is best for me. You, Lord, are the only thing that keeps me together; You are my glue. Not knowing You, I know that I would not make it. No one knows how hard it is for me and how hard it has been. I do not talk about it—only to You because I know You will not judge me and that You will love me unconditionally, regardless of the stupid mistakes I have made and will continue to make.

I am concerned about my children. I just plead the blood of Jesus over their lives and hope that one day I can be a blessing to them. I know I was a rotten mother sometimes, and I cannot do anything about it. I am so sorry that I put them through such a hard life. I am sorry that their father was not there as he should have been. I ask myself why I could not have done the right thing. Why was I a seemingly two-time loser in marriage? What is wrong with me, Lord? Why are my children struggling so hard? They are the most precious things in my life, and I love them very much. I hope that I can make it up to them someday and let them know how much their mother loves them. Somehow, some way, I am going to let them know that. As far as my husband, maybe one day he will not be my husband. At this time, I cannot say. So maybe that is something I need to realize that some things do not last forever. No matter how hard I try, it just might not last.

I am on my way to Fort McNair at the end of the week. God bless my son and me as we go on our way. Bless my job, Lord, and help me to be grateful and to always be prayerful about everything in my life. Help me to walk for my exercise each day after work and to focus on heaven. It sure is hell here trying to live right. Give me strength each day, Lord, and help me to live for You every day. Help me be a blessing to someone every day. Help me be a light in a dark and troubled world!! Your daughter, Rkh

December 17, 2003

Dear Lord, thank You for the vacations. Thank you for the cruises, and thank you for Hawaii. This is the best because I have grown so much in You. I love You, and I know You love me. I know this is all I need. I have a long way to go, I know, but I go willingly, faithfully because You have never failed me. Through all the hurt and pain from many situations, You keep me in peace. Thank You, Holy Spirit. Teach me to be even more content and peaceful, to crucify this flesh and the things that are no good for me. Put a covering over me, Lord. Lord, You are awesome, and more and more I realize that one day I will be glorified. One day, I will get my crown. I will live in Your presence and serve you "perfectly" one day when Jesus returns. I do not care who believes this, but I do, and I am a believer. I hope those who have ears hear and those who have eyes see! Thank You, Lord, for everything. Thank You for my future, because it is good. All things are good when you are in Christ Jesus. Order my steps, Lord, and you say, "I will. Just obey me and love thy neighbor, and keep my commandments." And the greatest commandment is LOVE! Thank You, Jesus. Glory to God. Hallelujah, Amen. Love, Rkh

February 7, 2004

Hmmm! We went house-hunting today. It was nice looking at the different houses. They were nice. Lord, I am still not sure what is right for me, and until I am positive that I can handle being in that situation again, I do not think I can do it. I mean, I know that we need counseling because I am resentful for the first seven years of our marriage, for the way he treated the kids and me. I have forgiven him for what the past held, but I am not sure the future with him will be any different. I know we actually love each other. I have no doubt about that at all. The question is, can we love each other enough and embrace each other's differences? I mean, we tried, and it did not work at all. We were under so much stress, and we became angry at each other and grew apart. But I cannot ever forget the times it was good. It was not just good—it was right, and it was love. We have had so many good times with each other, but not as a family. I can only remember a few. The other times were very hard, and those are the things I have to think about when making this decision. There is more to think about than just me and him. Lord, I need Your guidance, Your wisdom, and Your help. I do not want to make the same mistake again. God, it is a mess. Sometimes I just do not know whether I am coming or going. My life is in Your hands! I do know that You said that my later days will be greater than my past. So I am full of hope. I want to do what is right. I want to also stay married. I know we still have issues, though. I know we need counseling, because I do not think that I can handle this relationship unless we are both equally yoked!

God's Word says, "I will have that you will be equally yoked." It is not just about you and yours, baby. It is about ours and our God. I love You, God, and I just praise You. I have to be wise and seek God's face in this matter. Love, Your daughter, Rkh

February 10, 2004

A word from the Lord! I had a dream last night that I left someone, and it was hard, and some old friends were involved, and we (my children and I) had to strategically move out. We ended up almost getting arrested for drugs that an old friend had. She is an old childhood girlfriend; we were in the same old neighborhood. But we did not get arrested and continued to try to avoid the person (whoever it was) that I was trying to leave. We decided to all move together and start our lives over completely. I think we were going to my daughter's house, but I am not sure. I dreamed that we somehow got into an accident and a couple of friends got hurt. But I was still standing carrying my hurt friends and seeking help for them. One of the security guards was there where I currently work, and that made me realize that this dream was showing me something current for me. I am still standing and strong in the Lord!

My dreams are frightening sometimes, but I know that God is with me always. He said He would never leave me nor forsake me! He said I am more than a conqueror through Him. God's mercy kept me so I would not let go!

Lord, give me a clean heart and a right spirit.

Lord, hide your Word in my heart so that I may not sin against thee.

December 28, 2004

Wow! Almost a new year! Still standing. Thank You, Jesus!! Where did the time go?

April 10, 2005

Thank You, Lord, for another day and new mercies each morning. Thank you, God, that we have new mercies each morning because I know I ran out yesterday. New mercies—a reason to get up in the morning. A lot has happened since February 10, 2004. I got a job in California. My spouse (who was tired of his job anyway and had suffered a lot of devastating losses) was probably tired. His job situation was affecting his health, and he had been on sick leave for ninety days. He had no intentions of returning to his job. So when I got the job in California, he made the decision to go with me. Although I knew why, I did not say anything, nor did I really care. It would have been better if he had come because he *wanted* to be with me and make the marriage work (I have to be honest). But I know that it was because of all things he was going through and not because of me. If I had been the reason, he would have came with me the first time I relocated.

How can this marriage survive? Funny that it does not hurt as bad as it did before, and that is because I have come to the realization that my spouse closed (hardened) his heart after his first wife. Never to love again, I suppose, or maybe to love, but never to open up himself completely to another woman. Sometimes I wonder where I fit into the picture. I guess I asked for it, and I simply got it.

Lord, I wanted a relationship, and I sought after one, not even realizing that one should be very careful of what one asks. I loved him; he did not love me enough. He does not know how to love, and I realize that now. I pray that he will turn his heart to God, but he refuses. I do not understand, but I cannot just fall to pieces about it either. After so much loss, sickness, children problems, and relationship problems, I cannot imagine why I have not fallen completely apart. Maybe it seems unreal. Maybe it seems corny, but I know that it is because God told me that my later days would be greater than my past. I believe Him, and that is what holds me together. Even though I do not understand why I endure so much at the hands of my spouse, I wait. I am not stupid. I wait because I know His Word is true, and I need to just align myself underneath His will and wait and see what the Lord has done!! So I wait, and I do the best I can. Then I slip, and He picks me up and places me right back into His arms, accepting me all over again. What an awesome God we serve (swallow). That is why I continue on for God, for my children, for this marriage, for this world, for my mom, for my sister, for my grandchildren, and most importantly for my God's sake.

What is going on now is insignificant to what is going on in my spirit; my spirit knows all the good, the joy, the mercy, and the grace, and knows all about my problems. It sings and rejoices constantly. It is hard dealing with those who do not know this joy and peace. I just hide. Sometimes I do a very poor job (actually most of the time I do), but I know where my hiding place is, and I know I have to lean on God's grace and His strength. I do not have the strength to do this by myself. I have to demonstrate His attributes wherever I go. This is a lost world, and God has placed His children strategically in situations to make a difference in the name of Jesus. God is in control. I need to stand firm and just await the arrival of Jesus!

A lot of significant events have happened, and they are still going on right now. September 11, floods that killed thousands and thousands, the Pope's death, Prince Charles' marriage to the woman that he had an affair with during his marriage to Princess Diana, hurricanes, wars and rumors of wars, etc., just so much! Marriages are breaking up, and people are stone cold and selfish. There are so many things—children are lost, being mistreated and abused sexually, physically, and emotionally. There is pornography everywhere, yet we see so much advancement in technology, in the medical field, etc. The Bible says every generation gets weaker and wiser. Do not let me forget the Iraq war still going on, a senseless, seemingly never-ending war. When will it end, these countless things? People die unhappy, lost, confused, and never finding Jesus in their lifetimes (oh, I pray not). People are seeking countless ways to dull the pain of life's issues, searching and not finding hope. Seek Jesus! He will heal your pain. God is an awesome Father, and He will be your protector, counselor, mother, father, and lawyer, and will meet you right where you are. He is all that this world needs. Just try Jesus. Lord, I am so glad I did. If it was not for the goodness and mercy of God and His Son Jesus who died on the cross for me and my sins, I do not know where I would be right now. Keep me in Your will and keep me on my knees, oh God. I love You, God, Jesus, and the Holy Spirit. Love, your daughter, Rkh

August 16, 2005

Tomorrow is our tenth year anniversary. I am tripping because I have read back through the years and just wanted to shout "Hallelujah!" It was all You, God, and You are the only reason I have the strength I have today. We have been through so much. We tried counseling, and that did not work. He places all the blame for everything on me. Lord, I am very tired and yawning. I will write soon. Love, Your daughter, Rkh Thank you, Jesus!

September 10, 2005

Dear God, I love You, and I thank You for your loving kindness. That makes my heart fill with joy thinking of You and Your presence in my life. You have made a difference in my life. There is nothing in this world I yearn for more than Your loving kindness and tender mercies that give me peace and joy. God, I fall short and have fallen short so many times, and I thank You for your forgiveness. I cannot hold grudges or live in the past because of You and Your forgiveness. Although the past tries to haunt me, I know that it is not of You and that anything that is not of You cannot overtake me. I just go on. I cannot stand still I must press on. I am in the midst of changing jobs, hopefully soon. I know, God, that You and only You direct my path. Thank You, God, for promotions that come from You. Go before me and help me do what it is You would have me to do. Help me find godly friends. Your will be done in my life, not my will, Lord. Help me be a light to my children, to all my family, and to the entire world. I plead the blood of Jesus over this world, our government, our decision-makers, and everyone. I love You, God. Bless my husband, and please, God, open up his eyes to Your ways and Your will. It is very hard because of the facts and issues in our marriage. But I know that Your Word is that my later days will be greater than my past. So I wait, because I know God's Word is true, and He is able to do exceedingly, abundantly more than we could ever ask.

God, I ask tonight that You soften my husband's heart and open his eyes. Also, dear God, lest I forget, bless the people of Louisiana and Mississippi. Please, God, bless them and keep them and restore them and give them more than they could ever ask for. Bless the children, the parents, the sick, and the homeless. Lord, I know you are in control of this world. Let your light shine on them. God, bless all those who died in Hurricane Katrina, and bless those who lost family members on nine-eleven, and those who have lost their lives fighting the global war on terrorism. Bless all my family and the family members who have suffered losses in these tragic events. Bless this world with Your love. The most important thing that the world need is love. Help me to show love to all mankind. Fill me with love so that I can only show love. You are love. What the world needs now is love, sweet love; it's the only thing that there is just too little of. I love You, God, and thank You for all You have done for me. Love, Your daughter, Rkh

February 26, 2006

Today is my daughter's birthday. God, bless my only daughter. She is such a blessed young lady. I hope she knows it. She has everything: two beautiful children (my "grands," and I call them just that.) She has life experiences that will take her a long way. My daughter, like myself, has suffered tremendously on her journey. Someday we will hear from her. I know this. She has a college education, a zest for life and for mankind; I always have said that she is my humanitarian. Through all our struggles, I love my family.

I cannot believe it has been over five months, and I have not written. I always marvel at what I wrote before and how I got over and made it through and of the changes. I know You were there, God, and I take comfort in knowing You will always be there and when the time is right, You will show up and show out. I just smile. That is a funny term, because that is just what You do. Of all the things I have gone through in life, the ultimate victory has been mine. I would not change a thing. I often think when I catch myself getting deep, "Would I have changed a thing?" I think long and hard, and the answer is "Absolutely not." If I would change a thing, what would it be and if so, where exactly would I be? I am too afraid to dare to question God's plan for my life.

Well, I have changed jobs yet again and have gotten promoted and also finished graduate school. Thank God! I often think about getting my Doctorate, but right now, it is just a thought. I think a lot, but more importantly now I think of the why in everything. Right now, I am trying to answer the why in getting my Doctorate. I never wanted to gain anything for any selfish, self-righteous reason or for material wealth nor vain purposes. I only want to do God's will in my life. I have gone through too much, experienced too much to even desire to do anything outside of His will for my life. Sounds all perfect, right? Wrong. There are always obstacles and temptations, and the flesh that will try to rise up and defeat what is in your spirit to be achieved for the glorification of our God. It is a war every day just trying to understand the people around you, the things of this world, the hurt, the pain, and the why of it all. So although I talk a good game, some days I do not do what I should. That is when the voice of God says, "Press, press until the day of the Lord."

Some days, I go to bed very weary. Some days seem endless, pointless, and the entire concept of waiting and being patient seems ridiculous. But through everything I have gone through, I have learned that feelings change from moment to moment, from day to day, from month to month, and from year to year. So I continue to press. Some days, I want to give up and strike back, get even, talk ugly, and just plain do wrong just to keep my own sanity and that, in itself, is insane. Some days I say, "Is there *anybody* out there who understands?" But then, when I really think about it and compose myself, I know that it does not matter, because I know that I understand and I know that no matter what struggles or trials I encounter, I believe that God has directed my life and is in control and that His Word is absolute. He will do just what He said.

Completing graduate school is such a relief. Now I have some time to just relax and do some things I want to do. The new job is going fine, but my heart is back south, and hopefully, Lord God, You will direct me to go back in a few years. You know what is best for me. Please direct my path and give me wisdom—wisdom that I cannot say I have always had, but that I know has always been there for me to grasp. I have made some unwise decisions in my life, but with God, I know that I can deal with them. With God, I can fly high above any circumstance. The older I get, the better I understand about circumstances. We can live with circumstances no matter what they are, as long as we have God on our side. Some of the hardest circumstances we have to endure are because of our own decisions. I pray daily that I am wise enough not to succumb to my circumstances and continue to embrace the will of God. The fight is fixed, and we win (Israel). When we get to heaven, it will all be over. I would like for my God to say, "Well done, my good and faithful servant." That is more important than anything in this world to me. It is important to me to live right and to pick myself up and try to do it right again when I fall short. I am not going to complain about how hard it is, because I know what Jesus went through for us; there is no comparison. Although life sometimes seems so hard to bear, I must press on because I know that we have the victory; God's people, God's children have the victory. God says, "My sheep hear my voice."

Sometimes I wonder why I suffered so much in marriage, which at this time is my biggest concern. Some days, I just want to walk away. It seems too hard at times. The reality of it is hard to bear. But Jesus, I have prayed for my spouse and prayed that God would change his heart time and time again. I do not pray that God turn his heart toward me; I pray that God will turn his heart to Him. Because I know that when that happens, his heart will automatically be to me secondly. That is all I want. God first. Whatever our issues are, and I cannot exactly at this time put my fingers on them, I know that we still after all this time cannot come together on God and serving Him together in spirit and truth or our spirituality. Until that happens, I know there is and will be strife. It seems we both do better alone, but we continue to stay married. When we argue, we pull away from each other, and each time it gets harder and harder to mend the broken pieces. I wonder if it will last at least once a month. I wonder if I even want it to last anymore, or is it the determination that has driven me all these years to not give up keeping me here?

Sometimes our greatest strength is also our very own weakness, and we must find the proper balance. I believe in never giving up and to look for the best and embrace it and accept things we cannot change, find the courage to change the things we can, and the wisdom to know the difference. (I thought this even as a little girl.) The truth of the matter is that wisdom comes from experiences, trials, and with reconciling the inner being. That takes time. Oh, God, how we all wish we were born with that wisdom. The thing of it is that most of us, including myself, are well into maturity and thousands of mistakes later, before we even have the wisdom to know the difference. How profound, but we press anyway and do what we can and make the best of all things.

Back to my spouse and our relationship, I think there is a level of need that we both rely on each other for. As for me, I guess I just hate to see a marriage destroyed that could really be beautiful if we were equally yoked. If we both turned our hearts toward God and to each other, I know God would heal our marriage. That, in itself, keeps me determined to give it all I have—just the "what if" of it keeps me hanging in there. It is just like thinking, "What if Jesus comes today?" keeps me in focus. That, my friends is hope and nothing less—not living in a fantasy world. It is *hope!*

Some days are better than others. I know I am as much to blame as he is and hope that I am not trying to fill some emptiness or void through him. I heard our pastor say today that we cannot fill voids through a loved one. I have to address that and do some soul searching to see if that is what I am doing or trying to do. If so, then I know that I am putting too much pressure on my mate. I do not feel empty any longer since I found the Lord, and I definitely know God's love for me. I am happy in Jesus and have peace that I do not even understand myself.

No Date

Dear Lord, help me to find strength to read my Bible more and to go to the Wednesday night service as well as the Sunday service. I know, Lord, that I am completely lost without You. I need You every day just to make it through. It is hard being a wife, mother, grandmother, an employee, a coworker, and a friend and being Your child, God. It seems like so many hats to wear, and sometimes I get so tired of them all. Sometimes I do not want to wear a hat at all. That is when I bury my head under the cover and weep.

The drama in my marriage, at work, with the children, at church, with friendships, etc., is sometimes overwhelming. I am tired of dealing with those who say they believe but act otherwise and can or will not see the truth. I get tired of feeling like I am taken for granted, and like I really do not matter much. No matter what I do, there is not any appreciation shown, and the more I do the more is expected of me. To much is given much is required, not that I am doing what I do to get appreciation (I have long since reconciled that issue.)

God is love, and anyone who is in God is love and shows love toward others. I guess I have been on this soapbox for years in one area or the other. Maybe there is a level of resentment. I pray to God if that is what it is, that He deals with me about that and any resentment I am harboring. God is a forgiving God and has forgiven me for all of my sins, all those past and those to come. So please, God, if I am harboring any unforgiveness, please reveal this to me. How can I expect You to forgive me if I cannot forgive those who have trespassed against me? After all these years, nothing changes in the natural realm, but in the spiritual realm I can see clearer. I know God is always and constantly moving. Help me to be patient, Lord. The time will come, and I will come forth as pure gold. "Renew in me a clean heart and a right spirit." Thank You, Father God. Rkh

Afterthought: Bless my children; encamp Your angels all around them.

April 10, 2006

It is almost my forty-sixth birthday. Wow, I am maturing so fast! Funny, it seems like just yesterday that I was twenty-two. Oh well. I thank God for my age and more importantly for His grace and mercy. I also thank God that I feel great. Physically, mentally, and emotionally, I feel good ninety-nine percent of the time. When I get out of my Father's will and do not do the things I know that are right, that is when I am emotionally disturbed. However, as soon as I get back to doing what I know to do (church, prayer, reading the Word, etc.), I feel so much better. I love the Lord and I know that in this life we (God's people) will suffer. As long as we suffer for righteousness, God will see us through. God is love, and God loves His children. Lord, renew in me a clean heart and a right spirit. I love You, and please forgive me for all my sins, wrong choices, and the decisions I made without seeking Your counsel. I know that because Your Word says; "All things work together for good for those who love the Lord and are the called according to his purpose," I will be all right and I will come forth as pure gold. I love You, Jesus, and I will stand on Your Word.

Father God, please bless all my coworkers. We are working under a lot of pressure, and it seems that I am taking the bulk of the pressure, but I know that Your Word says that You will not put more on me than I can bear. I love You, Lord, and please give me the much needed favor I need at this time just to make it through the day. Lord, be with me each day and help me endure whatever it is that I need to help me be a better person and a soldier for Christ. I love you with all my heart. Love, Your daughter, Rkh

April 24, 2006

My sister's birthday passed, and I did not think about it until the twenty-third. I miss my sister so much. Sometimes I wonder what it would be like if she was still here. But, that is selfish, and I know that God makes no mistakes. It's just like me being here in this place that I am in now. Although sometimes I think I would be better off just being alone, I know that there would be the issue of loneliness and companionship. So I just endure. The Bible states that an ungodly man (or woman) is unstable in all his or her ways. I see the instability and, believe you me, I do not desire to be unstable in my ways. With God and only with God, I am stable, and it is only He who stabilizes me. I know within no matter what my actions are at times that I am stable because of God. I am able to love and care despite the fact that sometimes I want to run away when I have to deal with my issues. I am not perfect, but I do try to do the right thing in everything that I do and every decision I make. I know God knows and will work it all out for my good.

Sometimes when I sit in church, I want so badly for the Word to touch hearts and change minds and the way people think. The battle is not mine; it is the Lord's. Thank God for change, because if it were not for God, I would still be the same. Lord, have mercy. There is a rebellious spirit in this world against the things of God, and I do not know where that comes from. The devil is busy. I know most people care about the world and how the world sees and views them. It is so important to human beings to look successful and as if they have it all together. I know that no one has everything together, and I know God, and I know that deep down we all need Jesus to heal all our hurt and pain we keep inside. Whether it is from childhood, failed relationships, insecurity, or whatever, it is there and until we acknowledge that we need God to be whole, there is nothing we can do about our inside. We all need God. I know I do—even just to make it through this day. Lord we all need you.

April 30, 2006

The one thing I can say about my spouse, he does take care of his responsibilities, although the motives I question, but he does. He is a sincere man, hard-working, and is a very good lover. But as always with us since the day we met, when it is good, there is no better; and when it is bad, oh my God! I know it also has a lot to do with me as well. I have learned to be more patient, kinder, loving, and not internalize so much. I have learned to lean on God and not him for my strength. I have learned my true worth and my true validation, and it has everything to do with Father God and nothing to do with anyone or anything I have accomplished. It all has to do with the Father. I just know when God changes his heart, our relationship will be even better. God said He would not put more on us than we can bear, so I know that until that time comes, I can bear it. So, I am hanging in there just waiting for God to show up and show out! I pray that I continue to believe in God's Word. I pray that His will be done in my life and my family's life. I pray that when it is all over, God will say to me, "Well done My good and faithful servant."

May 10, 2006

I heard on the radio that we just cannot be saved and say we love the Lord. We need to be excellent in all our ways. Therefore, I know that I cannot be angry and mean in any of my situations. I prefer to receive my reward in heaven. Now, do I really mean that when the entire world wants to be rich, famous, on top, numero uno, to be applauded, loved and embraced by others, win the academy award, etc.? Although it is tempting and would be nice to show the entire world and to get back at all that have wronged me, taken me for granted, used me, laughed at me, did not believe in me, or treated me badly, I choose Jesus, and I choose getting my reward in heaven and not on this earth. My flesh may say, "Get it—come on, get it now! Get them back, fight back, curse them, and hurt them! Do not take it any longer." But I say (and I am the ultimate decision-maker of myself), "No, I will wait on the Lord" because the Word says, "Those who wait on the Lord shall renew their strength, they shall mount up with wings like eagles, they shall run and not be weary, and they shall stand and not faint." I will receive my reward in heaven. This is my choice. Thank You, Jesus. (I will suffer for righteousness). I love You, Lord. Rkh

Afterthought: I will go pray now and take communion. It is April 24, 2006, at 9:38 p.m.

November 10, 2006

I am reading this book I bought for a dollar at a yard sale in my neighborhood. I have read it once through and am going to read it over again as many times as I need to. God leads me to. The book is *Secrets of the Vine*, by Bruce Wilkinson. I know it was my time to read it and read it until I get it. I think about it all the time. It talks of fruit bearing fruit. I wonder if I bear fruit. I hope I do, especially with my family. I have not always acted well toward my children, my mom and sister, and my husband also. It is like I just do not understand them. I just want to shake them and say, "Life can be so easy." That brings to mind when Jesus says, "Pick up My yoke; My yoke is easy." But on the contrary, I wonder at times, have I actually practiced what I have preached? Have I picked up His yoke myself? The fruits of the spirit are love, peace, joy longsuffering, self-control, meekness, faith, kindness, gentleness, and all those adjectives that fit those categories. It seems I do well sometimes, and at other times I fall so very short. *Secrets of the Vine* is prompting me to take a closer look at myself in the mirror. I need this; I know I do. I feel like I am getting a breakthrough, and I need one so badly, especially in this arena. My attitude, tolerance, and patience have been unsatisfying to me. I have really felt that I am not producing any good fruit, and I know if I am so ill-mannered and grumpy, there is certainly an underlying problem that needs addressing. I need this. I know I do. I do not even understand myself sometimes. The smallest things just irritate me. I do not understand.

I enjoy God, His Word, His music and worshiping Him, talking with Him, etc. As long as I am in the spirit, I am so happy, but as soon as I walk out of it, it is like I am blindsided by others' lack of knowledge. I know I have to get control of that again. It has been a period of six months that I have been feeling like this. I know it is an attack of the enemy, and I pray that I will soon be able to combat this issue with my reactions. I feel like I am just plain tired of dealing with others' refusal to build a solid foundation with God. I feel like it is so unfair that I have to tolerate all this mess just because others do not desire or want to pursue the things of God or to change their selfish ways. I have given out so much and have tried to be the very best that I can be for everyone, and I feel like it is not appreciated— that I am taken for granted at times and actually used. Those things I would never do to anyone. I must admit I have been that way before in my life, but now I have changed, and I only desire the things of God in my life. I want to do right and be right and walk right. It is so hard, and I am very disappointed in myself for my behavior. I have no one else to blame but myself, although when I initially started, I was blaming others (as you can see in this book of memoirs). But I know that I am not accountable for anyone else's behavior and that I am only accountable for my own. I am sorry, God, and ask that You will meet me right where my need is.

December 12, 2006

On November 12, 2006, I walked away from my marriage. I knew at the time that we were arguing. Although we did not get physical, I knew that it was over. It would be the last time he told me that he did not care, and I accepted it. I looked at him one last time and said goodbye. I had not planned to walk out. But I did, and I did not look back. I have not looked back one day since, nor do I regret it. When you love someone, you will set him or her free. I set him free, and in turn I set myself free. The Bible says to seek peace, and that is what I am doing. Although it has not been that long ago, I am happy. I am on my knees constantly seeking my Lord's face. I am holding on because he told me my later days will be greater than my past.

February 1, 2007

I am pressing on and listening so that I may hear Your voice. Direct me and guide me, oh Lord. I need You. Order my steps. I have found my peace, and my peace is within me. I am happy and living the dream. I know that I am more than a conqueror through Christ Jesus!

February 4, 2007

I sent a 2007 donation today in the year of completion. God will finish what He started. The book will be revealed. Lord, give me direction and guidance in Jesus' name. God, please help me be obedient. Tuesday through Friday, I will be up at four a.m. to write, edit, and then pray until six a.m. Bedtime is nine p.m., with seven hours of sleep. The due date is June 30, 2007. Funny, that sounds like I am expecting a baby. In some sense something is definitely being birthed. Thank You, Lord, for everything. I know it is not me, but You that live inside me. To God be the glory.

June 17, 2007

I am finalizing my book. I am having some struggles in some areas. I do not want my book to hurt or put anyone down. I am writing because God gave me the vision years ago. It has taken a long time for this to come to fruition. His Word says, "Write the vision and make it plain." Along this journey, I have received so many confirmations to go on. I know God will see me through this. I am almost complete, ninety percent complete. It has not been easy. Some days are better than others. I am certainly not keeping the schedule I wrote on February 4, 2007. I have encountered so many obstacles, working late hours due to personnel shortages, writer's cramp, etc. But never doubt, it will be soon! It is so awesome to be this close to something that could possibly change your life forever. I know and I pray that God's will be done, not my own. I hope and pray that this book will be life-changing for this world—as profound as the change I experienced on February 13, 1992. This is inevitable. I hope and pray that it will be a bright light shining and hope for many people, that someone will see Jesus because of my struggles.

When this happens, I will give God all the glory and all the honor He is so worthy of receiving. I know there is no way I could have done this without You, God. You have blessed me in so many ways. You have kept me and sustained me through many hard times. I know in my heart that it is not me; it is by Your grace and Your mercy that I am able to complete such a project. Lord, have Your way in my life. Keep me grounded and rooted in your ways. Please Lord, keep me humble and keep me stable. Help me help this world. Almighty God, You are the Alpha and the

Omega, and You know the end. You have set me up for Your glorification, not my own. Please help me do this and be pleasing in Your sight all the rest of my life. You have told me so many magnificent things. Help me, God. I need You. I cannot do it by myself. Achieve the vision you have set in front of me. Your later will be greater than your past. It has been, Father, just as you have promised already. It is only the beginning. This is the end of the journey, but another has begun. I thank You, Father God. AMEN and AMEN. Rkh

IF
(August 9, 2007)

If I have a million bucks, I love you.
If I have not a cent, I love you.

If I am happy, I love you
If I am sad, I love you.

If I am well, I love you.
If I am sick, I love you.

If I am atop, I love you.
If I am beneath, I love you.

If I am surrounded, I love you
If I am alone, I love you.

If all people felt the same.
Ah! I guess that is what heaven proclaim.

What can separate us from the love of God?
Rkh

CONCLUSION

The challenging life issues forced me to step outside of myself and my strength and confront my past, present, and future. I embarked on an incredible journey toward spiritual development and finding purpose. My memoirs are a bold testimonial of change and the courage one woman found to make a difference. As a result, I answered the call to true purpose. Change is always positive, although as it is taking place, it may appear otherwise and can even appear negative. But with the proper focus, I hope that my readers will understand that change is inevitable and directed by almighty God. Please learn from one life that changed—it can be contagious! Thank You, Jesus!

SECTION THREE

INSIDE OUTWARD

"God, grant me the serenity to accept the things I cannot change, the courage to change the things I can, and the wisdom to know the difference."

Introduction

The final section is the results of change, the deep inner wisdom that changes can cause if we embrace it wholeheartedly. The direction of change is from the inside outward and never outside inward. The inside outward change will give us enlightenment and awareness of our inner being—the uncontaminated realization of who we really are on a deeper level. The outside inward form of change is unreal, temporary, and will not last. It is the ego, our own ideologies, and the desire for unwarranted prosperity in the eyes of our society, a misdirected idea of success. Just remember, change is always inside outward and for good if you believe in a higher calling in your life. He whispers, "Go and tell those who have eyes to see and ears to hear." This is the Great Commission. Thank You, Jesus.

CHAPTER 7

Footprints

I began to put my footprints on paper in the form of the preceding journal in 1998. I was maturing, and it was painful at that time. It was not easy. Maturity is never easy. Maturity is something we long for and resist. We long for it because it is necessary to accomplish the things we desire and necessary for development into what God want us to be. It is called our ultimate purpose, and some call it destiny. Without sounding pompous, I know that I have matured, grown, and developed. When I read my own words over a span of nine years (from 1998 to 2007), I follow my growth, my maturity, and my development. How awesome is that? Hopefully, readers will not focus on the painful places, but will see His glory and how He can sustain them through their deepest trials and pain if they only allow Him. Ultimately, my hope is that they will see God!

I cannot remember being disappointed in my youth, not early on anyway. I remember in my young adult life being disappointed sometimes. I do not know what anyone else's thoughts on disappointment are, but my perspective is that I should not disappoint anyone. The Bible speaks of letting your yes be yes and your no be no. I absolutely do not want someone to rely on me for anything and then I not follow through. I try very hard even now as a mature woman to do what I say I will do. Therefore, when someone I know disappoints someone or if someone is disappointed, I always wonder how the person feels who has let someone down. I wonder if they care, if it bothered them, or if they really tried. In most instances, since I am an optimist, I believe that they did all they could. I am not sure if that is true or not, but as I live and learn and embrace life, I have really come to the conclusion that it really does not matter. We are all responsible for what we put out there, what and how we receive what comes back, and more importantly, how we internalize it. I have come to the conclusion that people will allow you to do everything for them but have a point beyond which they absolutely will not go themselves. As long as the other person is willing, they will sit back and receive, receive, receive, even down to working your fingers to the bones for them, picking up behind them, doing everything imaginable for them. That is why we need to be real with ourselves and have a limit that we will not go beyond. We need to be able to say no, and that is enough, and let it be conceived any way the other person wants to conceive it. How many times have you ever done everything humanly possible for someone and all they could do was ask for more? There has to be a stopping point, or while they are laying back in the receiving mode, you are giving until you cannot give any longer. Some people are not willing to give back to anyone what they want to receive or return what they expect from others. We can end up doing things for other people that we know they would never dream about doing for us.

Human beings are funny creatures. I often have to laugh, and Lord knows if the Word did not promise victory, I would not do a lot of things that I do. I would love to give back what they have given or gave me. But we have to stand on God's promises. It is not easy. It is a very painful place, but we do what we know to be right because ultimately, we are accountable to God for our own actions. How nice it would be if everyone would know and live by that.

Who would know that I would go through years and years of suffering because of my lack of wisdom? I know it was my cross to bear, and although I did not like bearing it, I did, just as Jesus did not want to bear the cross, but He did it anyway, without grumbling or complaining. I was so busy asking God to bring me out that I did not realize that it was for me to go through. No one will ever do everything right. We will always get tired and sometimes weep. I now weep for the children with parents who are not there for them to guide them or who have abandoned them. I weep for the marriages, for the wives and husbands that do all they can do and for some reason just cannot reach each other, and they end up in divorce or going from one relationship to another. I weep for all the parents whose children are gone astray. I weep for the children that have to grow up in this world that sometimes will not embrace them, for the children who grow up and find out that this is a very cold world and want to return back to their youth, only to find that it is gone. I weep for the children that did not have fathers or mothers, because it takes two parents to raise a child and even then sometimes you do not know what or why the little one is doing what he or she is doing. I weep for a long-lost daughter that cannot find her way back home; I weep for the sick, the wounded, and the homeless. I weep because I feel like there is nothing I can do. I weep because I get so tired sometimes. I weep for those who cannot find love and those who find it and then lose it. I weep for mankind. I just wonder why it cannot be easier. I wonder why we just cannot find the right answers so that everyone can live peacefully together.

I wonder why there is hate, strife, murder, sickness, addictions, wars, terrorism, selfishness, disease, prejudice, etc. I weep for our leadership and wonder why anyone would even want the job. I weep for the poor and the rich, and for those who do not realize that ultimately we are all the same. Whether in lack or gain, we are all seeking and searching for answers. I weep because the rich look down on the poor, and the poor resent the rich. Where is the balance? The answers never come, and the conditions get worse. "What can I do?" I ask myself. I say, "Just be accountable for my own actions and let God do the rest." One day, we will all be in a peaceful place.

So I wait and wonder when that day will come and dream of having absolute peace. All we can do is rejoice in that expectation and keep the faith and hold on to hope. All we can do is look to our Father God. Sometimes, I feel like I am so far off. But then God gives me rest in my sleep and restoration so that I may do this thing called living. I'm hoping that instead of seeing what is wrong with the world, I can see what is right in God. I'm hoping that I can stand for what is right and that someone...anyone...will be able to see the God in me. Oh, how badly I mess up sometimes, and I have to be so careful because just one time, one incident could turn someone so far from God. This is the responsibility I feel, and it burdens my heart so much sometimes that I feel that I have to be perfect when I know that is impossible. To be perfect is to be Jesus. The life of a Christian is very hard. The entire world looks and stares, waiting to say, "Aha!" I cannot imagine what Jesus went through when I cannot even handle myself, and He had the weight of the entire world on his shoulder and still does. Jesus wept.

CHAPTER 8

A Life Worth Living

As I look back, I can truly say that I have lived a life worth living. Thank You, Jesus! I have worked hard and played hard. I have loved, and I have been loved. I have made friends, close friends. I have lost some good friends along the way—the best of friends. Some I still have, and some I have long since said goodbye to. But in every place, every job, every trial, every tribulation, with every tear, with all the hurt, I can truly remember a friend being there. I have always been a private person so only a few can tell you the intimate details of my life, and those of you who can, know who you are. But none can tell you everything. I bore that journey alone. That seems so sad, but it is not. Although not physically alone, but alone—this was my battle to fight.

I always thought it was a battle for my spouse, a battle to save a marriage, a child, or a friend, but it was a fight that no one could fight but me and it was a fight for me, myself, and I—my story, my journey, my testimony to share. Somehow God gave me the ability to laugh, to sing, to dance, and to move on no matter what came my way. Most of the time, I was the giver, for not too many times did I receive. I can remember very few from whom I received much. I was the encourager. Even when I did not feel encouraged, I always had the ability to put myself aside and encourage others. I guess that is why everywhere I went, I had and made enduring friends. I wish I could gather them up in one big room and tell them how much I appreciate them being in my life. They are what kept me going when I did not even want to. When they shared with me their sorrows, I cried with them because of my own. When they shared with me their heartbreak, my heart broke too. When they needed encouragement, I encouraged them and in turn encouraged myself.

As I go through my journal and look back, I see how much I needed these people who thought they needed me. We needed each other to keep going, to laugh together and cry together. There is nothing more precious to me than friendship and loved ones.

If you receive but one thing from this book, I hope that you understand that if I had really believed, I would have danced through it all. I would have known what the end would be without one doubt. I doubted many times, and at other times just was so perplexed that I could only focus on God. Had I not put my focus on God, I am sure I would not have made it—at times not even understanding that ultimately it is what our Father wants us to do. He does not want us to struggle. That is something we choose to do because of our lack of understanding. Is it easy? Of course not. But it is definitely possible once we arrive at that place of assurance in His Word.

What road we take and how long it takes is based upon our actions, our reactions, and our choices. The directions are before us. How well we receive the directions and follow them is up to us. Some of us need what we need, and it takes longer to get there. My hope is that everyone will get there and in the midst of the journey, you will dance and sing along the way. As you read through this book, I hope you dance or learn to dance through all your trials and tribulations, through pain and sorrow, and through all your individual struggles. I hope you still find the strength to dance. "I hope you dance..." It is one of my favorite songs for good reason! If you do, then you are living; and if you do not, I hope this will inspire you to hold on and keep the faith, and yes, you have my permission to dance.

Through all the heartache and tears, I learned to submit my all to the One above. I am not saying it would have been easier, nor do I have any regrets. All I know is that it is all about spiritual maturity and growth. We will grow and mature whether we kick and scream or dance gracefully. We all have a higher calling. It is not to say that if you dance through it, you will not feel it. It is not to say that if you sing, it will go away. It is to say I only hope you will understand that it is all for the good of those who love the Lord and are called according to His purpose—finding one's purpose in life and reaching those we are in charge of reaching and to teach those whom we are in charge of teaching. We are here for a purpose and not for selfish gain. We must stop internalizing everything and pampering our own selfish needs. We must look past ourselves and outside of ourselves to find that purpose. It will never be found within ourselves. If you are looking within, all you will find is an inner struggle. Purpose is never internal; it is found externally, outside our own will. As you find your purpose, I hope you dance.

CHAPTER 9

Reflections

ood for thought. As I reflect on marriage in general, the entire concept says, "defeated." To love, cherish, and adore someone whether
we are rich or poor, in sickness or in health, until death due us part
screams defeat. As I think about my marriage way back then, I think of
how young I was and how immature I was, both times. All I knew back
then was what I was taught growing up—my own little world that consisted of a mom and four siblings, a little town, several family and friends,
my own circle of friends, and my own experiences from birth to about the
age of sixteen. At the time, I am sure it seemed overwhelming and huge.
My horizon was not stretched until I was about fourteen or fifteen. As a
young teenager, we would go and visit my aunt in Philadelphia for the
summer. I guess all any child needs is a tiny peep at another way of life or
even a time away from the norm. That might have been my saving grace.
Visiting my aunt during the summer was exciting. She introduced us to so
many other things that we would have not been exposed to otherwise, like
Chinese food, Fifth Street, hoagies, theme parks, Atlantic City, etc. I guess
buried in my subconscious, I knew there were other things and other places
to go to explore, to try, to venture out to. However, at that time, I suppose I
did what most people did. I actually made some of my life decisions before
I explored or ventured out.

When I began to reach out and expand myself, I was already married
with children. Although it is never too late to expand, I often think if I had
done so before getting married and having children, I am sure I would have

probably made different choices. This is not about regret; it is about the reality of it all. What I brought to the first marriage was a small mind and a vivid imagination. I dared to dream of a better way and a better life. To my second marriage, I brought hurt, anger, and brokenness, and a determination that no one would ever mistreat me again or tell me what to do and how to do it. I came with a serious chip on my shoulder and something to prove. Nevertheless, things are the way that they are, and we are who we are, and the things we have done are just that—things that we have already done. There is no looking back, no regrets, just afterthoughts and hopefully resolve.

Marriage is very serious, but we often do not realize its seriousness until we are already in it. Those vows, we often do not understand until after we have already said them. But it behooves me not to tell anyone to think long and hard about what you have committed to and to whom you have committed. Yes, you have actually committed to another human being. But not only that, you have also ultimately made a commitment before God. That is the seriousness of everything. We cannot love another human being until we find out who we really are in God. Finding out who we are in God is finding ourselves and loving just who we are and who God created us to be, imperfections and all. To love oneself is to be able to love another. To love oneself is to be able to accept another. Often, we do not realize that until we are older and have stood the test of time.

Marriage is beautiful and can be beautiful if both parties are whole. Often, both parties are halves and only bring fifty percent to the marriage. Unfortunately, the parties might be one hundred percent at different times. Sadly enough, one party may not give but a small percentage. Therefore, the strain and burden becomes too much for one of the parties to bear, thus relationships end in separation. My word is that married people must look at the commitment and the vows and get the proper understanding of what it is they actually mean. All too often, this comes later in life. There are not too many cases where both parties grasp the dynamics of those two words, "I do." This is because we all grow and mature at different degrees and levels. Sometimes our understandings are different, and sometimes our upbringing and morals are different. Our views can be different, and our goals and expectations can be different. We look at the dream, and the dream is beautiful—"Until death due us part." We get married and try to live the dream. Often to find that dreams do not always come true. What happens next is dependent upon so many things. Do we stay, do we endure, or do we go? More than half of America chooses divorce. That does not count the separations or those who just live apart and never divorce. For others, the choice is unhappiness; for some, it is extramarital affairs, etc. But no matter where we find ourselves, we must realize that there is life after the "What next?" We must continue to strive on to press toward the high calling, that is, if we realize there is a higher calling. The higher calling in today's marriages is commitment.

CHAPTER 10

Judgmental Eye

I attended a conference this week, and it was awesome. It had everything: workshops, seminars, worship, music, guest speakers, etc. It was very nice. I attended alone. It was okay. I am alone a lot, even though I am surrounded by a spouse, children, coworkers, church members, friends, associates, neighbors, people in the mall, at the restaurants, grocery stores, etc. It is not the kind of alone that is negative, though. It is the kind of alone that is peaceful—alone, not lonely. I enjoy my time alone. I listen and write. I think about God a lot and I wonder what everyone else thinks and feels. Mostly, I hope that they can feel what I feel. But in reality, I do not believe that most do because of the state of the world today. I wonder why they do not feel the way I feel about life and God. It seems like a lonely place to be. But at the same time, I absolutely do not want to be in any other place.

There is a sweetness and a serenity inside me—a place no one can get to, a place where I need to remain all the time. It is a place I sometimes forget about and venture out too far, but quickly return to. No matter how far I go away from that secret place, I always return. I wonder; I ponder; I reflect; I dare not tread to far from that place. It is a safe haven for me when the world seems so cold. I cry in that place, I weep, I pray, yet it is the place where I get my help, my strength; it is where I lick my wounds; it is a comfortable place and a place of comfort. It is deep within my soul. It is a spiritual place—a place of rest. It is where I talk to God, and God talks to me. It is a place like a river that runs deep. It flows continuously and re-

174

freshes like a nice warm shower throughout my soul. It is a cleansing place of repentance, acceptance, renewal, and restoration. It is a place where I seek and search and look for answers. It is where I seek understanding, wisdom, and guidance. It is my roadmap to where I need to go, and when I go in the wrong direction, it navigates me back. It is an encouraging place and a place of victory. Be encouraged.

CHAPTER 11

Heart to Heart

My disposition, as I wrote earlier in my journal, was not good. It seemed I could have great days, and in public I was fine. I smiled and I felt happy. But when I was really reflecting on my behavior within closed doors, it was different. I felt unsettled, unhappy, and not satisfied with my behavior at all. I lashed out at whoever was closest to me. Even now, as much as I have prayed about my attitude, I still have to struggle with my actions. I think by nature I am a very warm and caring person. I definitely believe in doing what is right. I believe in everyone doing what is right, and that is where the struggle with the attitude begins. I struggle with others who do not respect rules or order and those that demonstrate a lack of discipline and self-control. I believe in reciprocity and treating people the way I want to be treated. I feel like I can change the world. Or at least I felt like that. I do not feel that way anymore because I know that only God can change a person. No matter how upset I get, no matter how I try to handle the situation, I am only human and ultimately not even capable of handling my own iniquities. Now that I know that, I still sometime feel mean-spirited, but I have so much self-control now that the majority of the time, I do not even bother. I don't lash out like I used to, and I am happier than I have ever been in my life.

I am a mixture of so many pastors and ministers and saints. When God came into my life, it was certainly not me feeling a little emotionalism and then the next day or month or year from then, nothing. From the time I gave my life to Christ, it was on. I began to change. The things I was interested in did not interest me any longer. It was strange. I had struggled with some issues prior to getting saved, but God dealt with me about them before I got saved. I knew right from wrong, and every time I did wrong I regretted it.

When I smoked, I knew I hated it and did not smoke in public. I was a closet smoker. I waited all day long for a cigarette, and as soon as I got home, I smoked my first cigarette. After the first one, I would smoke up until bedtime. So I knew I could probably quit, but I just did not. On New Year's Eve 1991, I made the same New Year's resolution I always had—not to smoke. This time, it was different. The desire was gone. By the time I got saved on February 13, 1992, smoking was not an issue at all. I have never smoked again. Hallelujah! Other things did not happen so quickly. I struggled with my attitude a lot. I struggled with understanding and wisdom. I thought I knew it all, and I did not. I began a journey—a journey I will now call maturity in God. The one thing I can say now is I never looked back. I never turned away. That is why I know that I was called. So many times, I slipped. But I never turned away from the love of God. I held on through thick or thin. I prayed, I attended church, I joined different ministries, and I attended Bible study.

I took my children faithfully also. I watched them grow and mature into teenagers that went to Bible School and attended Children's Church. I am extremely proud of that. I am the makeup of so many ministers and pastors and just good old plain believers. I am the Pastor Plummer, the Sister Thorton, the Graham, the Swilley, the Bynum, the Jakes, the Meyers, the Charles Stanley, the Price, the Evans, the Dollar, the Jones, the Hagee, the E.V. Hill, the Osteens, the Paula White, the Dukes, and many more. I have listened and been under and influenced by some of the most powerful ministers in the world. I know none of them personally, but they have all had a part of who I am and what I have become. They taught me so much along my journey, and hopefully that Word according to God is hidden in my heart that I may not sin against Him. It is funny that they do not know me, nor do I know them. I just know the face, the voice, and if I walked up to most of them today they would ask, "Have we met before?" That is the awesomeness of God and His power. I don't know them, but yet I can still be a part of what they know and believe.

I am certainly not saying that I believe every word that they have said or have stood behind every truth they have presented, but God in His infinite wisdom has given me from each of them a love, thirst, and desire to go on in His precious name. Through all the years at different times of need, they were placed there to ensure that I would never give up. What a friend we have in Jesus! Thanks, all of you so much, and keep growing people!

The maturing process is not easy. There is so much to learn and so many lessons. Sometimes it feels as if we are just not getting it, and then one day we know that we have it. There are no time constraints or time-sensitive lessons that we need to learn. It will take as long as we allow it to take. We cannot or will not move forward until we learn what it is God will have us to learn. That is why we all grow differently and all of our journeys are different. No journey is the same, and no one grows at the same pace. God is the Alpha and the Omega, the author and the finisher of our faith. No one can write a different story than what destiny holds. As I grew, it became harder to actually do the wrong things—not harder to get into things easier from that standpoint, but harder to feel satisfied in doing them. It is hard to understand, but those things I once ran to I still ran to them, only with a heaviness of heart and a repentant spirit every time. After a time, the total desire to do those things was taken away, swiped away, because basically I just got tired of feeling the heaviness and the burden.

Only when I reflect back can I actually identify that process, what it took to get where I am. Even deep reflection cannot pinpoint when the conversion took place. Only God knows that. I cannot identify when the exact moment was that I came out, but I just know I came out and that I made it through, and that is the ultimate goal—making it to the other side of through. The closest I can get is written in a form of a journal that I wrote in a nine-year period of time, at some periods writing faithfully and at other times not writing for months at a time; all I do know is that God was with me every day because I always came back praising Him and thanking Him no matter what the circumstance was or how bleak things looked. There was always praise, through the sorrow, pain, agony, confusion, anger, unbelief and so on, each time returning to my journal and giving Him His glory. When I grasped that concept, I grasped something worth holding on to.

All these words are not just writings—they are things that I learned through my journey. The journey taught me how to be and how not to be. I learned not to judge or esteem myself higher than anyone, but to live and let live because we are all God's children, and He made us all and loves us all. He died on the cross for us all. He endured until the end for all humanity. How much more shall we understand that we, too, shall have pain and sorrow, but we shall endure until the end?

He said, "Write the vision, make it plain, and they shall walk and not faint." If the Lord said it, you can count on it. He will do just what He said.

CHAPTER 12

Change

Throughout the growing up process, every day results in change; whether it is in appearance, noticeable, unnoticeable, sudden, or slow, it is inevitable. I learned that word—inevitable—a long time ago at a very young age. I often used it through my growing years as a young adult and even now. I always liked the word. Not a lot of people used it back then, but it came up in my conversations regularly. Sometimes people would look impressed, and sometimes I would feel like I had just spoken a foreign word. Nevertheless, I learned it and it stayed with me. Although it is not a very big word, it is a necessary word. Its meaning is powerful if you really think about it. Inevitable … it will happen … there is nothing anyone can do about it … incapable of being avoided or evaded … a situation where only one alternative is considered possible … foreseeable … predictable … to be expected … to be anticipated. That is what change is all about. Whether we welcome it or not, whether we resist it or not, whether we acknowledge it or not, whether we deny it or not, whether we think we need it or not, change will happen.

I sometimes wonder why we all have to change, but then I compose myself and remember that I know the answer to that question emphatically. We have to change because of the need for us to grow and mature. We have to grow; our bodies and minds have to grow. We have the period of growth in our infancy when we grow and learn at a rapid pace. Then, as youths, we develop and grow at a much slower pace, but this is when we are taught—we go from elementary school to high school and for some, to college,

180

growing and all the time changing our minds, our looks, our status, changing everything about ourselves—some by choice and some change that is inevitable. Through the years, we are continuously developing; our life experiences develop us, and our upbringing develops us. When we become adults, we continue to grow in our pursuit to take care of ourselves and our responsibilities. How well we do at this important task stems from all of the above. Nevertheless, there is growth. Nevertheless, there is change. We continue to grow as we go into maturity and through the aging process and hopefully develop maturity in God. Every day, we are growing, both mentally and physically. It is the reason we go through the situations, circumstances, hard places, tears, sorrow, and pain in our lives. It prompts and compels us to change. Sometimes change is forced upon us.

What direction we head in is entirely up to us. From bitter to sweet or sweet to bitter, we hold the key and actually direct our own paths. Through every decision we make and every choice we make, we are engineering our future and every step we make we are headed toward change. The ultimate plan is the Master's. The Master wants to put us together according to His will. Born into sin and with a sinful nature, we all go through the transformation into what we spiritually were brought into this world to do, to be, to birth, to help, to solve, to fix, to proclaim, to design, to propose, to declare…it goes on and on and on. It is in the Master's plan. We are here for a purpose, for a journey. That is why we seek and search, and we are never satisfied until death closes our eyes, and we are laid to rest. It is when we do not know what we are searching for that we get lost along the way. Hopefully, we will not get too lost before we find our way. Some have gone too far from home and have reached the point of no return. But for the most part, if we open up our spiritual self, we will be instructed in how to find our way back.

Our lesson in this is to welcome productive change and to defeat unproductive change. How easy, that is to say, as I look back on the many things I personally chose in my life that almost defeated me and sent me down the wrong path. There were challenges I had to overcome just to keep me going in the right direction. It was hard. Sometimes I was so blindsided that it felt like there was nothing else to do but to give up. In the times when I don't know how I got over it, I look back and I see. I shake my head in awe. If I had only known.

CHAPTER 13

In a Resting Place

We drove home from dinner with my daughter. I thought of her and how far she had come and the things she has overcome at such a young age. I thought of myself and my journey. This is her journey, and unlike me at her age, she knows the end. She will be a force to be reckoned with. I thought of all the children, and pride filled my heart, and I smiled a great big smile and belted out a loud "Hallelujah!"

As I continued to drive, I thought of all the things that could have happened and all the things that would have happened had I not had grace and mercy. I began to thank God for everything He took me through and thank Him for inspiring me to write. If He had not inspired me to write, I would not be able to share such an incredible journey, nor would I be where I am today. Where am I today, you ask? In a resting place, reaping all the benefits God promised me way back then. He said my later days would be greater than my past. To God be the glory!

CONCLUSION

Ultimately, the story ends with triumph and victory in every challenge that the character has endured. From all the trials and tribulations, hurt and pain, the result is the courage to make a difference. In the end, the character finds purpose and understanding of what life and having faith in God is all about.

I asked God often, and still do today, to please allow me not to be distracted during this quest and to help me see things with spiritual eyes. The things He has set out for me to do and say are eternal. I always thought of a some day (over the rainbow), but someday is here and now. Everything is done in His time because He is the Father of time. He created time, so therefore everything happens in His infinite wisdom. As I conclude this book, I understand that His timing is perfect. For the vision is yet for an appointed time.

I praised the Lord through the rejection, the pain, the trials and the tribulations, and He allowed me not to be offended. He whispered often and ever so softly in my ear: "Do not carry the load of offense; learn, grow and fly. Offense will keep you from fulfilling My will. I need you to speak My will into existence as it is in heaven." "Your will, my Lord?" I ask. He said, "For everyone to find salvation and to not just stop there, but to find purpose. Amen and amen." He saved a wretch like me.

Discussion Questions

1. How do you think EC will touch lives? How did it touch your life?

2. Who would benefit from reading EC? In what ways will they benefit? Was EC beneficial in your own life? In what way/ways?

3. Did the character handle her pain differently in the beginning verses than in the ending? How?

4. Do you think there was one defining moment in her change or many? Name the defining moment or moments.

5. Do you believe there is a need for change in everyone's lives? Why? Is there a need specifically in your life?

6. Is there ever a point where there is no longer a need to change? If so, when? If not, why?

7. Whether positive or negative, do you think that change is necessary for growth? Does there need to be both positive and negative change? If so, why?

8. Does anyone like the challenges or seemingly negative things in their lives? What role do challenges play in our lives?

9. What part did the character's beginning play in the ending?

10. Does the beginning always define the ending?

ABOUT THE AUTHOR

Rhonda was born and raised in Goldsboro, North Carolina. She currently lives and works in northern Virginia. She is a Senior Program Analyst for the Department of Defense (DOD) and has worked for DOD for more than 22 years. She holds a Bachelor of Science degree in Business Administration, majoring in Accounting, and a Master's degree in Public Administration.

She is married to Timothy and has three children and two step children. She loves to travel with her spouse and walk their dog. Her ministry is to promote inner change and encourage all believers to trust in God and understand that change is for the perfecting of the saints according to the Master's plan.

Rhonda started writing at a very young age. She feels that she inherited her passion and ability to write from her mother who wrote articles for their home town newspaper. She also gives tribute to the many great books she has read over the years. After finishing graduate school and as her children were getting older, she began to type her memoirs during her free time. As she did, a story began to unfold before her, thus leading her to write *Ever Changing*.

She is adamant about where her direction and guidance came from and hopes that everyone who reads this book will not focus on the painful places, but focus on God and how He took her from childhood to adulthood to purpose. To God be the glory!

CONTACT INFORMATION

For contact information, the author's blog site, schedule of events, and to schedule an event, please visit the author's website at:

www.e-rhonda.net or email everchanging@e-rhonda.net